16

WHY WRITE?

Self and Soul: A Defense of Ideals

Why Football Matters: My Education in the Game

Why Teach? In Defense of a Real Education

*The Fine Wisdom and Perfect Teachings of
the Kings of Rock and Roll: A Memoir*

The Death of Sigmund Freud: The Legacy of His Last Days

Why Read?

Teacher: The One Who Made the Difference

*Nightmare on Main Street: Angels, Sado-Masochism
and the Culture of Gothic*

Literature against Philosophy: Plato to Derrida

Wild Orchids and Trotsky: Messages from American Universities (ed.)

*Towards Reading Freud: Self-Creation in Milton, Wordsworth,
Emerson, and Sigmund Freud*

WHY WRITE?

*A Master Class on the Art of
Writing and Why it Matters*

Mark Edmundson

B L O O M S B U R Y

NEW YORK · LONDON · OXFORD · NEW DELHI · SYDNEY

Bloomsbury USA
An imprint of Bloomsbury Publishing Plc

1385 Broadway   50 Bedford Square
New York   London
NY 10018   WC1B 3DP
USA   UK

www.bloomsbury.com

BLOOMSBURY and the Diana logo are trademarks of Bloomsbury
Publishing Plc

First published 2016

ISBN: HB: 978-1-63286-305-8
          ePub: 978-1-63286-306-5

Library of Congress Cataloging-in-Publication Data is available.

2 4 6 8 10 9 7 5 3 1

Typeset by RefineCatch Limited, Bungay, Suffolk
Printed and bound in the U.S.A. by Berryville Graphics Inc., Berryville,
Virginia

To find out more about our authors and books visit www.bloomsbury.com.
Here you will find extracts, author interviews, details of forthcoming
events and the option to sign up for our newsletters.

Bloomsbury books may be purchased for business or promotional use. For
information on bulk purchases please contact Macmillan Corporate and
Premium Sales Department at specialmarkets@macmillan.com.

To James Naismith and His Game

Contents

CONTENTS

Why Write?

Why write?

Why write when so many forces in the world seem pitched against writing?

Why write when it sometimes feels that so few people really read? I mean read slowly, tasting the words: read deliberately, as if their lives might be changed by what they're reading.

Too often now the public reads for information, not enlightenment. People read to be brought up to date and put in the know. They want telegraphic bursts of prose. They want the words to be transparent, not artful or arresting. They need to get right to the truth, or failing that, directly to the facts. It can seem now that writing is a service: the writer dishes up information the way the counterman dishes lunch at the fast-food restaurant. In his worst moments, the writer feels that the world doesn't really want writing: if by writing you mean thoughtful, nuanced interpretations of experience that could actually shift some basic perceptions—maybe even change some lives.

And if that is the case, why write? Why try, with as much selflessness as you can, to enlarge the contours of your mind—and to give others what real writing always has: pleasure and instruction, beauty and truth?

The world wants to be informed not enlightened, and the world wants to be entertained not inspired. Fiction writers now are supposed to give the readers exactly what they want. Novelists are to provide well-crafted, modest explorations of modest but badly crafted lives. Poets are to speak of themselves and themselves only (no big reach—no justifying God's ways to man, or man's to God) and speak in a timid whisper of a voice. To be a poet in America now is a slightly shameful condition, like having a mild drug habit or talking occasional smack to other people's kids.

In America what once were artists are supposed to be entertainers. They shouldn't offer tough or potentially dispiriting work to the world: they need to shake their rattles and jangle their bells. They live in a culture that measures success by the number of copies sold not the number of spirits touched. They have to shorten their sentences and compress their sentiments to the common bandwidth. They ought to stop worshipping low-sale losers like Virginia Woolf (a suicide) or Herman Melville (died in despair) and begin to model their careers (writers now have *careers*) on palatable entertainers.

Get this straight, too. In America what once were essayists and critics are now consumer guides. They write not to tell us what art *they* favor. That would be elitist and narcissistic to boot. They write to let us know what we would like. They are in position to reflect taste (our taste) and not to shape it. They must use small neat words; they must pretend to like what the mass of their readers do; they must never make anyone feel dumb.

The artist is a glorified entertainer; the critic pens consumer reports. Under these conditions: Why write?

Why write when every day words seem to mean less and less? We are, it's said, becoming a culture of images. Developments in video technology have created wonders. A flat-screen TV delivers a vision that can seem more real than reality. The soft green landscape out my window can't compete in intensity with the high-def football game playing on the TV just below it. On the screen, life seems to be on fire. Every figure and every object appears to exude internally generated light. At the movies, we see that directors can put any image they wish on the screen. Dream it and your dream comes true. Would you destroy the Earth? Say the word to the special effects team, seated like obedient gnomes at their computers. Will you restore it all before the end of two hours? Done.

How can writing compete? How can shadowy etchings on the surface of soon-to-yellow paper or bug-like squiggles on a screen touch the glittering image? The TV producer has become a demiurge. The film director is Jove. How can the inch-ling scraping along with his stylus ever compete? It's an open question now whether any traditional art can have the impact of the most modestly produced and conceived video diversion.

And if that is so: Why write?

There is another simpler and perhaps more serious objection to be made to writing. There is already too much of it. We live in a torrent of words that are already written and words fast coming into being. The Internet has made everyone a furious scribe; that much is understood. But beyond the Babel of words that flows daily into the world there is the accumulation of the most distinguished words—the best that has been known and thought. Libraries overflow with them and the Internet, for all its excesses, has brought us within a few strokes of *Paradise Lost* and *Regained.*

Why write when Shakespeare has already written? What has already been composed and is now there in the public domain is daunting in its magnificence and plenitude. An entire lifetime isn't enough to read all of the literature in English, or English translation that is worth reading. More lifetimes would be needed to take in the best of the sciences, law, social thought, and political reflection. Why try to add one's bit to this amazing horde of words, a treasure we can now see and enjoy online, with less exertion than it took the Arab merchant to whisper "open sesame"?

And why write when it is so damned hard to do? There really is no writing, one is told time and again. There is only rewriting, and in this there is some truth. The ones who have come before have set the bar high and every writer knows that no matter how lucky a day it has been, how smoothly the first draft rolled out, there will still be dozens of revisions and re-revisions. Writers often look at what they have done and say simply: "It doesn't work." When a mechanic says as much about the engine, he usually knows what's wrong and what needs to be done, or he can narrow it down to three or four possibilities. But the writer often has no comparable clue. It's broken; she knows that. But what's the fix?

Walt Whitman implicitly compared writing to the work of "a noiseless, patient spider." The spider is constantly sending strands of filament into the void to create his web. Sometimes the strands catch and hold, but mostly they don't. The spider, undaunted, keeps letting the filaments flow. Whitman's suggestion is clear enough: the writer's efforts come from deep inside, out of his guts. When he fails, it is not language that is failing or the genre or the culture: he is the one who is failing and it is (dare one say it?) very much like a spiritual failure. Yeats says it as well as anyone ever could:

A line will take us hours maybe;
Yet if it does not seem a moment's thought,
Our stitching and unstitching has been naught.
Better go down upon your marrow-bones
And scrub a kitchen pavement, or break stones
Like an old pauper, in all kinds of weather;
For to articulate sweet sounds together
Is to work harder than all these, and yet
Be thought an idler by the noisy set
Of bankers, schoolmasters, and clergymen
The martyrs call the world.

Yeats is right (and amazingly eloquent) but I doubt the lines have ever changed the mind of a single banker or priest about the writer's lot.

Writing is backbreaking, mind-breaking work. So, one might readily ask: Why bother?

Why write when the work is as lonely as it is? A writer is isolated in two senses. There is the obvious sense: she works all day (if she can) and she works alone. There is usually no one around to talk with; there is no one to complain to after you've bored your wife or husband near comatose for the thousandth time. We're told now over and over again that human beings are social animals. Life is about the group. People who don't have a thrumming circle of friends and don't get out much are the ones who grow readily depressed. They become anxious; they entertain poison thoughts; they find themselves stuck with all the maladies that loneliness brings. We're now disposed to think collaboration is the name of the game: The best products are team efforts. Hit TV shows are created by committee. It takes a village to raise a child and it takes an army to make a film. Let's pool our talents. Let's all have a say. Let's put it to a vote, then e-mail and tweet until we've arrived at revelation. Meanwhile, the writer slogs on in her slightly toxic and highly suspect isolation.

There is the literal isolation of the writer: a room of her own can become a private cell, to which she's somehow lost the key. But the writer also takes her isolation into the world. Browning calls the poet God's spy and that's a complimentary way of putting it. We could say, more neutrally, that writers are almost always spies and have the kinds of lives that spying creates. They are constantly collecting information, making mental notes. Henry James said that often the foundation for a tale or even a novel of his was "a glimpse." A woman steps out of a tram in tears; an otherwise well-dressed man has holes in his shoes. In a crowd, writers are by themselves; at the party they may laugh with the group but often seem, both to themselves and to others, to be laughing alone. Once they've committed themselves to the writing game there is always a measure of detachment. Whitman said that he—or the part of himself that mattered most, the Me-myself—was never fully present. He was perpetually "in and out of the game and watching and wondering at it."

People live to achieve total absorption in the life around them: they want to be immersed in happy circumstances and feel calm and contentment. They find this state with their families, with their friends, watching a ballgame, or playing a round of golf. Writers out in the world almost never seem to achieve this condition; they are always watching and wondering at it. They rarely manage to disappear happily into their own lives. The only time most writers can reliably get in sync with themselves is when they are writing—and then only when it's going supremely well. Outside the study (the cell) they are prone to feel that life is out of joint. And inside the cell—there they are alone, too.

There are so many reasons not to write and so many of them good: So why?

Because writing is one of the best acts a human being can turn his hand to. With all of these objections on file, and more besides, the case for writing remains overwhelming. Writing is a great human good, even a higher good than most of its best-known and most articulate advocates have told us. I mean real writing of course: writing that rises from the desire to give other people pleasure and instructions. I mean writing done with as much detachment from desire and purity of motive as possible. (Though no one could ever ask for that purity to be complete.) Ludwig Wittgenstein famously said that the limits of one's language were the limits of one's world. By coming up with fresh and arresting words to describe the world accurately, the writer expands the boundaries of her world, and possibly her readers' world, too. Real writing can do what R. P. Blackmur said it could: add to the stock of available reality.

There are plenty of bad reasons to write, and I'll be talking about them here. But mostly this book focuses on what seem the best reasons for giving oneself over to writing. Writing to make money and writing to possess the status of having written won't do much for you in the long run. But that's not all there is to writing. Writing can enlarge the mind and strengthen the spirit. It can improve character (if you let it). The process of writing can make you happy—or get you as close to happiness as people of a certain disposition are likely to come.

Writing—to highlight one of its benefits—can teach you to think. Doesn't everyone know how to think? Can't all of us reflect? We human beings are called the rational animals after all. But no, the truth is we can't. There's jumble and senseless rumble in our minds most of the time. We live in a stream of consciousness, and that stream doesn't always go much of anywhere. Writing disciplines the mind the way hard workouts discipline the body. Writing compels us to reason and to give reasons. Then, after we've written we have to go back and check our work with a cold eye. We have to strengthen what's weak and reframe what's faulty. We strive to *make sense* as the saying goes. The saying touches on a truth. For sense is made not by coercing the facts or pumping up the rhetorical volume. Sense is made by sifting through the sand of our ignorance to find, here and there, the words and thoughts that persuade ourselves (truly) and perhaps consequently to persuade others.

I'm not sure how, without writing or intense conversation, we could ever learn how to think. Oh, we could learn to plot and scheme, all right. As human beings we are driven by desire—and usually we choose to try to satisfy that desire. So the practical mind comes into play, sometimes fiercely. But I persist in thinking that one hasn't really lived unless one has tried to think about a matter that doesn't touch on one's own immediate profit. We may never answer grand questions about human nature or what the best way of life for a man or woman is, but we are at our best when we pursue such questions. And to think well, we must train the mind much as the athlete trains the body. I sometimes think that to have been born with that majestic faculty, the mind, and have never truly thought and written is like having been born in our bodies but spent our entire lives on a mattress: no sports, no sex, no dance, not even a leisurely walk across the park.

Writing is thinking; thinking is writing. But if that sounds like too gray and utilitarian a reason to make writing part of your life, or to live for writing straight out, there are other reasons for writing that are of a more delighting sort. For once you're at home with words there are few more pleasurable human activities than writing.

"How do I know what I think until I see what I say," says E. M. Forster, and this is probably true of many of us. We don't know our views until someone asks us. Writing is a way of asking ourselves. What comes out can be dismal: it's true. Whenever I try to write something about American politics I'm forced to remember that the political is something I'll probably never understand. Is it all about the needs of selves, or collections of selves? Does soul ever enter in? Does something like a spirit of benevolence? I never know where to begin. Though at least I know that I do not know, which the ragged philosopher Socrates thought a good enough condition to spend his entire life endorsing.

But sometimes, for everyone who writes, words tantamount to wonders pour out. Truth comes forth: or at least the truth that is true for you. And sometimes the shivering soul who says never—never could I write a poem or conceive a play—by sitting down and putting a word on the page then another discovers that there are worlds inside him he never knew. Is it good? Is it bad? Sometimes it's enough if a piece of writing simply *is*. It is. *It is and I did it.* Through writing people can sometimes say along with Wallace Stevens's persona in the marvelous poem "Tea at the Palaz of Hoon": "And there I found myself more truly and more strange."

Who am I to write a book about writing? What qualifies me to take on this difficult matter? I suppose I could point in the direction of a stack of books, a few sheaves of articles; I could flourish an advanced degree or two. But really, I think what chiefly qualifies me to write about writing is that I've been a slow learner. I've gone by small steps. I didn't publish a book until I was nearly forty and I drafted that one so many times that when it was done I felt like I'd written ten. But traveling by foot has its advantages. You get to look around and take in the territory, see where you are and plot out where you're going. Maybe taking the gradual overland route has put me in a position to be a guide for others, to help them out in ways that those who have flown over the same ground in a gleaming silver jet never could.

This book is organized around themes: writing and memory, writing and thought, writing and sex, writing and fame, writing and (cue the gnashing of teeth) being reviewed. But it's also a lightly drawn writer's autobiography. I start with issues and events that dominated my early period of writing (or trying to write), move through some meaty midphase issues, and end with thoughts about the writer's later life, at which I've now more or less arrived. Writing can bring your mind to birth—and it can also let you carve your own tombstone if you're so inclined. And in the middle years, writing can help you reach many other goals, infinitely worth reaching. So here it is: some autobiography, some inspiration (I hope), and even a dose of how-to.

There's so much to be said about writing (real writing, I mean) and in the pages to follow, I'm going to say some of it. I'll draw freely from the great ones who came before me, and of course add something out of my own experience. Many wonderful words have been written about writing—words about the joy and pain of composing words—and I'll rely on some of them here. But I'll add something to the mix, a thesis if you like. As much praise as writing has gotten through the years, it has still not gotten enough. We are still not entirely aware of what writing, good writing, can do for individuals and for the collective. We have at our hands' reach a skill that is also a spiritual discipline. Writing is a meditation; writing is as close as some of us can come to prayer; writing is a way of being, righteously, in the world. And this is something that everyone ought to know.

GETTING STARTED

TO CATCH A DREAM

FOR A LONG time, I tried to figure out how I was going to get started as a writer. I knew that a writer was what I wanted to be—though it wasn't clear exactly why. Surely it was in part because I was certain I'd never be very good at anything else. But how was I going to get started?

All right, I'd done some writing. I'd composed some essays for my college classes and those had been received well enough. But assigned writing wasn't really writing. Writing, I thought then (I was about twenty I suppose), was something you did because you wanted to do it, maybe because you had to do it. It was a form of self-expression and it was self-initiated, not commanded by anyone else. Writers were "self-begot, self-raised, by [their] own quick'ning power." Or so I believed.

I began carrying a notebook with me everywhere I went. I was waiting for lightning to strike. And sometimes something did strike. Though on examination it always proved to be something that didn't really qualify as lightning. I'd get an idea for a story, some lines for a poem, a concept for a movie script (I wasn't particular; I'd start anywhere). But then I'd think about it. This? This is going to be the *first* entry in my writer's notebook? This is how I'm going to get my start as a writer? It's too thin, too clichéd, too boring, too trite, too something or other. This can't possibly be the way *I'm* going to start.

Is it possible that I was thinking of posterity? Could I have conceivably believed that future scholars would find my first scratchings and connect them to my later work? Maybe I was thinking of Keats, whose juvenilia has traveled with him through literary history like a broken can on the tail of a dog. *Vanitas. Vanitas.* I had a bad case of it. What more is there to say?

But how bad could these early ideas of mine have been? I can show you, because as it turns out I remember one. It came in the form of a "poem." I concocted it sitting on the front steps of my parents' house in Melrose, Massachusetts. And on first consideration, I thought it pretty darned good. I had my notebook with me at the time. (I had my notebook with me at all times.) I even had a writing implement, a pencil as I recall. I reached into my pocket, pulled out the notebook, which was not imposingly made. It was not a leather number with my name engraved on the front, or even one of the sternly bound black items they sold at the bookstore of my college, where they were much in demand (for many of my contemporaries were poets; some were visionaries). No, mine was a much-sat-on pocket-sized once-royal-blue notebook, with a spring across the top that had sprung loose and looked like a strand of unkempt hair from a very curly head. Had it been red, it would have been a spring of Raggedy Ann's. My pencil was a pencil.

I drew forth the notebook and flourished the pencil and there, sitting on the doorstep of my parents' home in Melrose, I took a long breath and tried to begin to begin as a writer. It was just before dinner. The sun was more out than not, but it had put in a solid day's workmanlike performance and was ready to set; the grass had been cut (though not by me—allergies and indolence); and the birds from the cemetery down the street were gathering (they must have been, since they did this every fair-weathered day at the same time) in a massive oak tree beyond the cemetery wall, a tree that no doubt knew the secrets of the ages, having seen (maybe) Pilgrims and Indians and even a stray Salem witch or two.

Nature held its breath, or at least I did. I looked down, addressed the blank page, the white ghost-like page that haunts writers, or haunted them constantly until its job was taken by the screen of a computer that contains inside it news of the world, sports clips, pornography, and many other diversions: I addressed the page and I wrote absolutely nothing. That's what I wrote: nothing.

And it's not hard to understand why. What I had in mind was a poem. It was an untitled poem, inspired probably by all the existentialist philosophy and fiction I had been reading in college. The poem, or anti-poem, or non-poem (yes, I think that's it), ran this way: "There is a deity at the essence / of which, of what, I know not. / Only this: that the essence is lost."

Somehow I was both very proud of having concocted this and fully aware that it was abstract, boring (if you can be boring in three lines you truly have a gift) and ridiculously pretentious. Yet I was proud of it. And yet I knew it was vile. Knowledge defeated narcissism—and I wrote: nothing. A few days later the empty notebook disappeared and beyond school essays, which were tough for me to compose as it was, I wrote nothing for oh, two or three years.

The moral of this story is pretty clear. I should have torpedoed my doubts and written my pompous lines. I should have made those words my beginning and the hell with it. Starting takes guts. It usually means putting something down, looking in the mirror that is judgment, finding yourself ugly, and living with it. If a fool would persist in his folly he would grow wise, Blake says. And sometimes he is right. But I looked and I was scared and I ran away like the timid kid in the horror movie who manages to get slashed or gobbled up anyhow. I went cold and icy and dead. He who desires but acts not breeds pestilence, Blake also says. I ducked down that day and bred a little pestilence in myself, the pestilence that comes from wanting to do something worthwhile and being too timid to stay at it.

It's surprising how rarely accomplished writers are willing to talk about their initial efforts. Or maybe it's not: sprinters are never game to tell you how hard it was for them to learn to walk. Robert Frost tells a melodious story about how he "made" his first poem. He spent all day making it he says. He became so transfixed that he was late to his grandmother's for dinner. "Very first one I wrote I was walking home from school and I began to make it—a March day—and I was making it all afternoon and making it so I was late at my grandmother's for dinner. I finished it, but it burned right up, just burned right up, you know."

It's well told. (Frost always tells his stories well.) But it smacks a bit too much of the Immaculate Conception for me. I like Frost's other earthier story of where his poems come from. It's as though, he says, you're walking down the street in your hometown and coming toward you is a fellow you've known all your life. You and he are fond enough of each other—though not too fond. What you usually do when you cross paths is to exchange insults. And this time you see him before he sees you, just a moment or so, and on the back of your tongue (I elaborate a bit here) there arises the taste of the most tangy, civilized but nasty insult you've ever conceived. And it feels good and when the time comes the delivery is a perfect strike. You score, 1–0: point, game, match. They tell you that you don't have to score, Frost says. But you do. Today, with your insult you do. And that's what it's like to make a poem. "It's him coming toward you that gives you the animus, you know. When they want to know about inspiration, I tell them it's mostly animus."

That day sitting on my parents' porch, watching the grass go golden green in the twilight and aspiring to Keats-like thoughts, I imagined that writing came from the impulse toward sweetness and light. That's the impulse Frost seems to attribute to himself in the first example. I wanted to summarize the world for the world and lament its sorry state in detached and compassionate terms. A deity at the essence! Alas, the essence is lost.

But I should have realized that writing doesn't always come out of pure motives, at least not at the start. (Though I think that finally it's best when it does.) Writing can be analogous to playful insult (or semiplayful), to invective, to curse, and to rant. Milton, Blake says, wrote best when he wrote from Satan's vantage. The Puritan poet was of the devil's party without knowing it. It's necessary early on not to idealize the process too much, or to idealize yourself. (Though later on there's room enough for high aspirations.) You want to get a sail up, even if it's a ragged one, and plunge into the bay. I jumped in, Keats says. Rather than staying on shore and taking tea and comfortable advice, I jumped in and maybe made a bit of a fool of myself with *Endymion*. A critic named Croker laughed at

Keats. But who has heard of Croker now, beyond knowing that Keats's friend Hazlitt called him "the talking potato"?

I think that eventually writing should be about truth and beauty, right and justice and that it should seek to profit others more by far than the writer himself. But get in by any door you can. Keep composing the lachrymose sonnets, full speed ahead with the "proud bad verse" (Keats again, though from the later, better *Fall of Hyperion*). Forward march with the inelegant essays; spring off the line on the first hut with the miserable rewrites of *Les Miz*. As long as you can in time recognize that they are bad and need work and that you must (and will) get better, you are triumphing. Virginia Woolf said that you should never publish anything before you are thirty anyhow. But get rolling now, even if you are thirteen (or seventy).

I wonder sometimes how many aspiring writers there are wandering around in writer limbo, hoping to make an august start, unwilling to touch pen to paper or finger to keyboard until they have achieved the inaugural mot juste, the Flaubertian word for just exactly right. I wish I could reach out to them and pat them on the shoulder and tell them it'll be all right, and that there is no time for starting like now. Take some courage from me. Take some spirits. And if you're truly desperate, I have some inaugural lines never really used that I offer gratis. Start with them if you want. "There is a deity at the essence. . ." From here, there is nowhere to go but up.

So how did I start? How did I get to the business of writing? I owe it to Hunter Thompson and to the invention of the electric typewriter. And oh yes, to drugs: I also owe it to drugs.

At a certain point in college I became enamored with the writing of Hunter S. Thompson. Thompson was the gonzo journalist par excellence who steamed himself up on drugs and wrote wild, scabrous, trenchant pieces on Richard Nixon, the Hells Angels, and other outlaws in American life. (Nixon and the Angels really do belong on the same page.) The archetypal photo of Thompson shows him bent like a vulture over his typewriter, long neck in a downward curl, bald head poised over what looks like a meal of bad meat but is really an exposé on Greedheads or that swine of a man and jabbering dupe of a president Richard Milhous Nixon. In his eulogy for Nixon he averred that the former president's body should be burned in a trash bin.

Everywhere Thompson went in America he experienced fear and loathing and tried to create some, too, through the engine of his prose. He was a mannered fellow, actually a bit of a dandy, with his cigarette holder and his tinted yellow sunglasses and his bald dome before bald domes a la Michael Jordan became the thing. He looked manly, more manly almost than Hemingway, who did all he could to fuse writing (a lady's parlor game, the fellas feared) with grand-safari masculinity. Hunter even had the right name: he pursued big game with the avidity of a trained woodsman.

He also spent much of his time high as a monkey, or at least his persona did. He suggested that without a closet full of drugs—uppers, downers, sliders, smackers, and blasters—there would be no writing from Hunter S. Thompson. He wrote the way Andretti drove a race car—full out, balls to the walls, into the wind. Later on I'd learn that Hunter was a bit of an eleven-year-old, living off and alone near Woody Creek, Colorado, getting high and shooting off guns and going *wow*. And I'd also learn that when he was just starting out as a writer, he spent his time copying page after page of Faulkner and other writers to see how it was done. Nothing especially gonzo about that.

But what my twenty-three-(or so)-year-old self got from Hunter Thompson was the image of a guy who fueled himself like an expensive engine with high-octane drugs, threw himself down in his writing chair like a bull rider hopping on the brahma, then opened the chute (which is to say wrote a word) and let the bucking start. Thompson (my Thompson) wrote the way Rocky Marciano fought. Full out, throwing everything he had into it until covered with sweat and maybe bleeding from the nose, he flung his hands over his head—victory!—and collapsed in a winner's heap. The man went at it.

I was not Hunter Thompson to be sure. And even then I had an inkling that Hunter Thompson was not Hunter Thompson either. But I followed his lead, or what I imagined to be his lead, and threw myself into writing sessions the way I had thrown myself into playing football: all out, head up, and body on the fly into the tide of the oncoming.

I had a Hunter Thompson sort of subject at my disposal, too. I was working as a stagehand and security guy at rock shows outside of New York City at the time and my life was full of rock bands and drugs and bikers and girls who stood up in the crowd partially clothed and danced to the music the way serpents do to the charmer's pipes. I'd seen riots and backstage fistfights and a knifing (maybe). I'd watched (from under the safety of the stadium eaves) as a Hispanic street gang heaved down lumps of concrete on my front-gate security crew, like the denizens of a medieval town fighting off attackers. (Get under the eaves, you dopes!) We had refused to let the gang in for free (or I had), even though the concert was taking place on their turf and so they were expressing their sentiments. To complete my Hunter Thompson experiential bacchanal, the Hells Angels turned up for our Grateful Dead shows. One show got canceled because of foul weather even though it said "rain or shine" on the back of the tickets. The Deadheads rioted. (One would have thought they were too stoned to manage anything as active as rioting, but they proved proficient at it.) The Angels ascended to biker heaven when it became clear they were expected to put down the riot through any means they wished. The image of a large Angel standing at the front of the stage urinating down on the Deadheads clambering to get up and destroy Jerry Garcia and his guitar and steal his drugs (presumably) is one I won't forget and one that seemed sent by the gods when, a few weeks later, I sat up late in my linoleum-floored room on West 187th Street, up near the George Washington Bridge, trying to get it all down.

I pulled a complete pseudo–Hunter Thompson. I opened an envelope full of white powder—which might as well have been talc from the pool room, so potent were the powers of suggestion alive in the air—laid out a long sequence of lines, turned on the electric that had been willed to me by my writer buddy Michael Pollan, and I went to work. I wrote for seven hours running—Thompson hours—flying full force, headlong breakneck, amok in drug and sports imagery. I did not stop typing except to roll in another slice of yellow paper. I hit the keys so hard I blew holes in the yellow sheaves where the *o*'s should have been. It must have sounded like an all-night gun battle.

And from time to time I'd look down as if from a great height and say to myself, "I'm writing. I'm writing. I am writing!" It was like learning to ride a bike. It was like nailing three-pointers one after the next from the corner. It was like getting the hang of sex—if one ever gets the hang of sex. It was like magic.

I was so happy with what I'd done that a few days later, after a cursory redraft, I sent the manuscript—spilled on, fat, and sloppy as a pile of old bills—to George Plimpton at the *Paris Review*. (Michael and I had taken turns working there, basically failing to sell ads for that distinguished journal.) I knew for certain that Plimpton would love it. He'd been into the experiential journalist thing before Thompson even, though he was a bit too much of a white man—Exeter, Harvard, Hasty Pudding—for my newly fledged wild self. I did not think much about the response that was coming from Plimpton. I more or less figured that after my burst, publication was a done deal. I could now get some more ideas and write more.

What had happened? How had I finally—if a bit absurdly—done the thing I so much wanted to do and could not? How had I managed to begin, or at least begin to begin? Well, I'd made myself into something like a battering ram—a heavy, fast-moving force—and I'd rammed my way through my inhibitions. The inhibitions were a well-made, heavily cemented wall of rocks and even boulders. I was quite simply afraid that my stuff would be terrible. I was afraid that I'd see that I had no talent. I was afraid that deprived of my writing ambition I'd have no other ambition remaining and be left wandering in the void.

So it took a lot of horsepower—some of it manufactured, some of it absurd—to break through. I had to pretend to be a guy I was not. And from what I could tell, he himself spent a good deal of time working on his gonzo persona, pretending to be a guy he was not. I had to counterfeit a counterfeit. I also needed the audience of my two roommates who stayed half-awake that night in awe of my amazing dedication to the craft. And the drugs! Later on in grad school I'd settle for coffee to get my writing done—so much of it that in time it part ruined my stomach. But this time I needed the devil's dandruff, as Robin Williams illuminatingly called it. Though I expect it was more the outlaw feeling of cutting those lines and laying them out that amped me than the drug itself. My roommates turned up their noses at it—which meant it was poor quality indeed. And perhaps it was truly nothing but talcum powder. (But coke: a deathtrap. We didn't know that then, so stay away!) To write what I thought to be the truth (my truth!) I needed fictions, fabulations, creative swerves from reality, dreams! But I started writing that night and from then on knew I could at least participate in the game. I might never be a *writer* like Hunter Thompson, but I would write.

So many young aspiring writers out there—or older or simply old straight out—escape the trap of silence any way they can. One guy I know did it by putting a woman's name at the top of the page and running free; one by dictating his tales; one by three days' meditation preliminary to the first, first draft; another by putting the pencil in his left hand, his off hand, and grinding it out. To get started you can use any means necessary, though crazier means probably won't work over the long run. Pretend, pretend, pretend, if you have to, in order to get to the real.

You're breaking out of jail. If you do it digging with a spoon, that's fine; if you trick the guard that's OK, too; maybe you simply have some rich friend buy the dungeon and turn you out. By any means necessary. Because once you're out, you're out. A toast to you—my hand greets yours.

The rock-and-roll piece? A month later I got a letter back from George Plimpton beginning with the words: "It's not very good. At least not publishable." I walked around in misery for a while, feeling as put-upon and resentful as the Count of Monte Cristo when he left the dungeon after the years of wrongful imprisonment. But like the Count I also felt free. I was out and I was on my own. I was writing.

And Plimpton was wrong (give or take). My riff about the Grateful Dead show and the Angels anti-riot rioting did get published, albeit after a bit of revision and some patient reconsidering. It's in the first chapter of what in many ways is my favorite of my books, *The Fine Wisdom and Perfect Teachings of the Kings of Rock and Roll*. So what if it took thirty years to see the light of publication!

Often a benign invisible hand presides over these matters. Hey, there's a deity at the essence, right?

TO DO IT EVERY DAY

WRITERS—ESPECIALLY WRITERS who write books about writing—tend to do a lot of talking about the blank page and lately about the blank screen. It's a frightening prospect this blank space—looming up at us like the void. Every day, in a manner slightly heroic, we have to enter this void and make it pregnant with feeling and thought. Daunting of course: scary, harrowing. Each morning (or if one is prone to stay in bed as long as Dr. Johnson and a few others did, every afternoon), you've got to rise and fling a lance at your own version of the great white whale: the pale, empty page.

Well, that's overdoing it of course and writers—and especially when they're writing about writing—tend to do that. They like to make of the regular encounter with their work something rather epic. Male writers are especially prone to this I suppose, often wanting to make of the writing game something within hailing distance of war, or at least lion hunting. We don't always like to think of Jane Austen, sitting in a room with her family, her page beside her needlework, chatting and sewing, and by the way creating the most exquisitely tempered sentences to be found consecutively in English.

But there's truth buried in all the whale-hunt-style hyperbole. Writing is *hard.* It's tough to get up every day and have the wherewithal to sharpen the pencil or hum up the machine, and then set in. How does one do it? How is it achieved? How do you go from being, on any given morning, someone who is not writing to someone who is? Even after you have *begun* as a writer, you must every day contrive to *begin.*

Virtually every writer I know has a ritual or, to play it down a bit, a routine that guides him or her into the act of setting words on a page. (Page: yes, for a while let's stick to the old idiom.) One claims to sharpen half a dozen pencils to start; another gulps down a can of beer (before noon?); a third meditates (the sound of chanting from up in her lair gets the kids scrambling off to the school bus—that noise is *embarrassing*); a fourth needs espresso; his cousin requires Darjeeling (or not a silent verbal peep will be made) straight from China; a last goes outdoors and marches for a while to the beat of a different drummer: marches, literally, around the backyard.

What these rituals prove is that you've got to have an entry strategy, a way to open the door. But where exactly are you when you begin? And where are you trying to go? And why are there so many different keys with which writers open what amounts to the same door?

If you're a beginner, how the heck do you find the key that rightly belongs to you and to the door that happens to stand between you and your dream of writing every day? "We think of the key, each in his prison," says Eliot. "Thinking of the key, each confirms a prison." It's beautifully eloquent and no doubt with multiple applications. But on the matter of writing there is a prison (self-enforced silence) and there is (I think) a key. Though each person probably has to grind one to fit his own lock.

Even after you've made the grand initial leap—as I did I guess with my Hunter Thompson masquerade—there's still the work of getting up for it and into it every day, or at least five days a week or so. On the matter of how often to write, I'm a follower of Stephen King, who says he only takes off Christmas and his birthday. I take off Christmas, Christmas only. (He just writes faster than I do.)

These writers' rituals: what exactly are they for? Some people simply like the idea of being eccentric and so they try to be. They're home alone, working alone, and they can ignore office-like protocols and cultivate a little weirdness. But I don't think most writers' rituals are mere affectations. I think them quite necessary. The writer needs the right room, crowded or bare; the right drink, soft or mildly spiked; the right ambient noise or a dose of earmuffed silence. And the writer needs a way to go from what I call (borrowing from Keats again) habitual self to some other state.

There's nothing wrong with habitual self. It's a state we need to inhabit most of the time, unless we're saints or warriors or artists who never stop creating. (Picasso seems to have come as close to this condition as any mortal ever has, and even he needed to pause for some food and more than occasional fornication.) Habitual self drives the car and gets bodies, including its own, to various places at agreed-on times. It gathers the groceries and chops them and marinates them (though if cooking is truly an art, maybe habitual self doesn't *always* cook the dish). It pays bills and takes care of kids and parents and schmoozes at the post office. It takes the obligations related to death and taxes with some degree of seriousness.

But habitual self cannot write to save its life. Habitual self is good for a grocery list, a laundry list, a note to the mechanic, or a note of thanks for the spotted birthday tie or the fruit-scented candle. But habitual self cannot write. It is worldly, pragmatic, geared toward the fulfillment of desires, and fundamentally boring—at least to others. At base, habitual self is the Darwinian side of us that wants to survive and thrive and procreate. When habitual self wants to read, it reads Grisham; when it wants to write, it sounds like a machine. It sounds the way your computer would sound if it had a voice of its own.

I think sitting down to write is about getting loose from habitual self. If you're going to tap into what's most creative inside you, you've got to find a way to outwit the pressures of the ordinary. Think of habitual self as a barrier that blocks you from getting where you want to go as a writer. It's not that massive wall that most of us have to smash through to get ourselves going the first time and make ourselves able to say we've *begun* as writers. It's a smaller, less imposing but still potent version of that wall, and it rises up to some degree every day.

There are two ways to deal with that wall I think. You can go over it and you can go under it.

Most of the people I see and work with every day are professors; most of them write. And when they prepare to write they usually gear up to go over the wall. They attempt to speed themselves up. They rev themselves internally until their minds are whirling at a higher velocity than they habitually do and with the strength that speed brings, they leap the barrier and they begin to write.

And like all writers they have their rituals. Not surprisingly, those rituals tend to be caffeine based. They drink two or three (or five or seven) cups of the strong stuff and it helps them burn through their inhibitions. Their fingers itch, smoke pours out of their ears, they taste gunmetal in their mouths. They feel confident, a bit aggressive, focused. And so of course they usually write in an authoritative way, which is more or less what they want.

I understand the desire to leap over inhibitions—to try to Evel Knievel over the wall. It was more or less my method through graduate school, when I used to come off a bout of writing sweating like a prizefighter. I had barbells on each side of my chair—heavy ones—and when inspiration flagged, I pumped them, up and down, up and down, until I was back at fighting pitch again.

I took this form of getting started to an extreme: along with the barbells there were hideous amounts of coffee and occasionally a small white pill that will go unidentified.

And I think this way of starting, this flying over the wall, works for a lot of people, including people who don't think all that much about it. They drink a cup of coffee, then another and another, and they set to work. It's a ritual really, but by now it seems simply like a routine. Writing is tough and whatever works, works. But I'm tempted to say that writing that begins by speeding through habitual self is fraught with dangers. It tends often to be two-dimensional and bureaucratic sounding: linear, flat, and unsurprising. To use Freudspeak for a minute, you're turning yourself over to your superego, the inner agency of authority and command. Whatever you can say positively about the superego, it's not genuinely a creative agency. (Unless you mean creative in the ways it can torment us. Then it can get pretty flashy.) Left to itself the superego powers through in search of a potent and univocal truth. That may be the kind of writing some people want to produce—editorialists and bosses and policy experts and theorists of this or that. And it's probably a good thing to be able to produce writing from above when you need to (probably, maybe). Though when I see all those kids (people under forty) sitting in Starbucks and juicing their screenplays and novels while hypercharged on java, I fear for the future of entertainment.

I prefer writing that slips *below* habitual self and taps other regions of mind and spirit. But getting there is probably a little more complicated than drinking three cups of black, or buying the full display case of Red Bull and rationing it to two, three, four—OK not more than five cans a day. To fly under the radar of habitual self, and its harsh older brother, authoritative self, you're going to need some skills of a subtler sort.

I think most of the best writing comes not from staying pat (habitual self), or speeding it up (authoritative self), but from slowing it down and making contact with a dreamier, more associative part of the mind that—if you connect with it just right—will in certain ways do your writing for you. You can fly over the radar on coffee or speed (or in-chair barbell pushing), but flying (or cruising) under it is more complex.

How do you slow yourself down? I think you've got to hypnotize yourself a little. That writer who loves to sharpen six or even a dozen pencils before she starts is, I'd bet, using a repetitive action to get a little way into a dream state. That's what's going on too, usually, when a writer does some meditation. (It's not that hard to learn. The Gita teaches us the rudiments, right down to what kind of animal skin we should slide under our bottoms.) The idea of meditation is to calm habitual self and get it to stop planning and worrying. (Habitual self loves planning of course and can go into ecstasies of worry.)

You can charm habitual self to semi-sleep with music, too. Though you need to find the right kind of tune to get you started. I especially like the *kirtan*—chanting—that a deep-voiced, spiritual-sounding fellow named Krishna Das, KD to his admirers, can do. Most of KD's chants have about five or eight words in them and those are in Sanskrit—making it easy enough for me to hear hypnotic sounds rather than words. I don't usually continue to play music once I've gotten started, though a lot of writers do. I tend to lose my own writing rhythms in the rhythms of the music. If I play anyone while I'm writing it's often the glorious jazz pianist Bill Evans. Evans is melodious, clean, and original in his riffs in a low-key, non-show-off way. He never overwhelms you. His music is almost kind; you might even call it understanding. Ah, if I could write the way Bill Evans plays! But mostly I save Bill for early evening and try to write in the flow of my own inner music, such as it is.

Get under the wire, get under the garden wall, and see what happens. The romantics believed that the unconscious mind was a creative mind. Coleridge brought the idea of the unconscious over from the German romantics: the term is *Unbewusste* and Coleridge and most of the other major British romantics believed that tapping the unconscious could produce wonders. In his own case, Coleridge may have been right. His Unbewusste (along with a dose of opium) seems to have given him the beginnings of his weirdly majestic poem "Kubla Khan"—which for whatever reason, the Unbewusste declined to finish.

You don't have to believe in an apocalyptically creative unconscious to believe that making contact with the part of the mind that produces dreams (and occasionally unexpected jokes and—recall Frost—tangy insults) can also help you produce good writing. Of course there are dangers in trying to go under the wall, just as there are in flying over it. Listen to too much chanting, or do too much on your own (yes, I sometimes chant along) and you may find yourself falling asleep and waking up refreshed but guilty at the end of your allotted writing time.

But there are subtler challenges, too. Get a little too deep into the twilight state and writing loses almost all shape and direction. You commit automatic writing—more illuminating to your therapist than to a reader. You want to be at least two-thirds awake and alert to write, and that's usually not so hard. The simple physical act of typing or scrawling or cursively lettering (if you're that much an aesthete) will probably keep you in the game.

The members of the health service complex are always going on about the value of a good night's sleep. But it's possible, just possible, that they are not really talking to writers and other artists. I often find that when I've slept too well, I have trouble getting through to the more creative side and getting on with my work. After I've slept miserably, I may start out bleary, but once I get going I'm often more fertile than when I've had a standard good night's rest. Maybe a big deep sleep gives you lots of room for dreaming and that satisfies the unconscious well enough. When morning comes, the creative spirit doesn't need to come forward: it's done all it wants to during the night. I know by now that when I sit down to the computer or the pad feeling jagged and cranky, I may well be in for a good writing day.

Anyhow, I suggest you skip the coffee and leave the black beauties on the shelf and see what comes out of a lazier, calmer approach to getting writing done. Go for a run first—a long run. Have a dropper full of valerian in water. (But watch out. It's surprisingly potent for a drug they sell at health food stores.) Chant, meditate, chill by any means possible. Then see what turns up.

The key to all this is to find the approach that unlocks writing for you. It surely varies from person to person and even for a given individual it changes over time. Somehow the door gets moved, or the old key gets rusty, or the landlord (god Apollo?) changes the lock. A lot of trial and error can be involved. But it is trial and error of an interesting, I might even say revelatory sort. There's something to be learned about yourself as you find what mode of shifting consciousness works for you. Writing involves a bit of shamanism, in which you're both guiding shaman and space-traveling, time-traveling subject. What you need to travel tells you something about your version of habitual self and also about the kind of writing you're born to do. And it demonstrates your resourcefulness in getting to the place you need to be in order to do it.

There is, according to some, a guaranteed way to shift consciousness and to slip into the zone. This method not only gets you into your game, but it also does much more. If what its devotees say is true, the method will get you writing as you never have before. It will help you pass through the gates of habitual self (that's a given) and also enter the empyrean of brilliant ongoing creation. Through this method (if method is truly the right word), you will be re-created and that re-created self will be something of a miracle for all to encounter and (more importantly for our concerns) for all to hear and to read.

The method I have in mind doesn't involve drugs, even of the most potent sort, unless you think of matters metaphorically.

It surely doesn't involve religion and it doesn't entail magic, though its effects, we're told, are magical enough.

I mean falling in love. Not just any love of course—you've got to fall in love with the man or woman who is your soul mate. This is the person who completes you and makes you whole: the yin to your yang, the moon to your sun, the day to your night, and all the rest. When you meet the one, or the one who is the one for a while, your powers are augmented. You breathe in a little truth and light; you see, as Wordsworth put it, "into the life of things."

Percy Bysshe Shelley seems to have felt that he could only really write when he was in love and what he wrote when in love was majestic. My grad school prof Harold Bloom called Shelley "the most intense and original lyrical poet in the language," and I agree. To Shelley, being alive meant being in love and he was in love almost all the time. ("I always go until I am stopped," he said of himself, "and I never am stopped.") In the state of being in love, Shelley wrote *Prometheus Unbound* and *The Witch of Atlas* and *Ode to the West Wind* and more and more. He was, as all true romantics are, inspired by Eros. It breathed new life into him as nothing else could. And he seemed to breathe new life into his beloved, too. Mary Shelley wrote what's probably the most potent and adaptable sci-fi myth we have when she was in love with Percy: *Frankenstein*.

Did I say Shelley's beloved—beloved, singular? That's not quite right. There were many: Mary and Jane and Harriet and others, too. He loved them with fervor; they inspired him and he them. But he was also inclined to leave them when the inspiration ran out. That's the downside of romantic writing; the love runs its course (a little like a fever) and the inspiration disappears with it. Then it's on to a new beloved. The fire needs fuel. Shelley left plenty of human wreckage behind him, as well as the miraculous poems.

But it works, or at least it worked for P. B. Shelley and Keats and Blake and Coleridge (in a way) and rather weirdly for Wordsworth (who loved nature as though it were a living human being, reveled in its powers to inspire, and feared that it would in time "betray the heart that love[s] her"). Love inspires Hart Crane and Allen Ginsberg and Bob Dylan and Joni Mitchell, and thousands of rockers male and female and in between. Though rock—and a certain sort of romantic poetry—can also be all about tearing down the perceived illusions of romantic love. Who can hear the J. Geils Band's magnificent "Love Stinks" and not be at least temporarily moved?

"As high as we have mounted in delight, in our dejection do we sink as low," says Wordsworth. He's not talking directly about romantic love here, but he could be. After the rhapsodies of discovering the soul mate and reveling in the powers you impart to each other, there almost inevitably comes the fall. You drop out of phase with each other: she loves another; sickness intervenes; death. The aged archons, the patriarchs and matriarchs of convention, get in the way: "Your papa says he knows that I don't have any money," cries the frustrated lover. The papa in question is the papa of the (probably fictive) beloved of Bruce Springsteen, the immortal Rosalita. Springsteen outwits papa: he has a new record deal and just got a big advance. But does it always work out so well?

The writer who relies on love for day-to-day inspiration is taking his chances. Some of us, the Wordsworth types, need a long, long time to recover from erotic failure or loss. Others, the Shelleys among us—if any still exist—bounce like a flaming ball from love to love and never touch the ground, much less dunk beneath the flame-eating waves. If you are one such: All honor to you! Beauty and light and truth and good times may be yours.

If not: meditation, chanting, the ritual sharpening of the pencils. Or coffee: have a cup of coffee if you really, really must.

THE NEW WRITER

TO HAVE WRITTEN

"THE TRUTH IS," a friend told me when we were young and in the habit of going around telling people that we wanted to be writers, "the truth is I don't really want to write. I want to *have written*." It took me a while to figure out what my friend meant, but eventually I got there.

Even at the time, he was something of a young gentleman. He had an apartment with bay windows; he had what qualified as a small library worth of books, the majority of them hard-backs; he occasionally, and without any provocation I could discern, put on a bow tie of lepidopteran elegance. He had a lovely girlfriend. He was a bit of a dandy, but a very bright and industrious one. Still, he did not so much want to write as to have written.

He wanted what he imagined as the life of the writer. He wanted to spend a lot of time in New York (we were trapped in dowdy New Haven) and to attend cocktail parties with people from *Partisan Review* and *Paris Review* and the *New Criterion*. He wanted to appear on panels; he wanted to be on TV to comment on the cultural emergencies of the day; he wanted to be invited to benefits and sit at head tables and schmooze with dignitaries. He wanted to have Carlos Fuentes's phone number in his book and to call Susan Sontag "Susan" and Gore Vidal "Gore." (Who can blame him about Vidal, who had a dash of real wit. Asked to be godfather to the child of friends, Vidal replied, "Ah, always a godfather, never a god.") My friend would have wanted to be able to call Robert Lowell "Cal." (If he was an up-and-comer now, he'd want to be the first guy in Brooklyn to get a beer with Martin Amis. He'd want to have been loused up once or twice, but not too fiercely, by Emily Gould.) He surely wanted to appear in the *New York Review of Books* both as reviewer and reviewed—and for this honor he was willing maybe (just maybe) to do a little writing. Still, Bartleby-like, he would greatly prefer not to. Perhaps for Robert Silvers, the esteemed *NYRB* editor, he would be willing to dictate something.

When he went to a party he wanted to be recognized. He did not want to be pointed at across the room (it would not be that sort of party), but he did want to be known from his TV appearances and from the cover-sized photos on the backs of his (already written) books. He wanted what Freud said all writers want: fame, wealth, and the love of beautiful women. He wanted fame in particular. When I told him he already had some share of these prizes (he had a rep as a brilliant student and teacher; his girlfriend really was wonderful), he would scoff at me and tell me I knew nothing of the world.

Perhaps he was right. When I thought of the life of the writer, which I very much wanted, it was something out of Balzac. It involved a five-story walk-up, crumpled balls of paper, and ink all over my hands. It involved many rejection letters and a girlfriend who threw crockery. I imagined I would commit some rather distinguished works that would be roundly ignored and some tissue paper efforts that would succeed. (Not long before, I had betrayed a shocking ability to compose a respectable *restaurant review*.) I didn't want to have written. I wanted to learn how to write, and to write something more lasting than a prickly dismissal of some poor restaurateur's escargots. "You know nothing of the world," my friend informed me when I told him my aspirations and anxieties. I had trouble disputing him.

My friend—who turned out to be quite a literary success, though alas he actually had to write to become one—was closer to the common mark. Many, many people wish to have written. They know writing to be work, especially in the early phase when one is learning the art. (In my experience, the early phase can last about ten years.) But when they have written, they believe that they will take on a new, larger identity. People will look at them with awakened eyes. Their daytime aura will glow more brightly. At noon they'll cast a bigger shadow. Face it: human beings want respect and then more respect, followed by adulation. Writing a book can still count as a way to cop some of the esteem we require. It's been said that to survive all we need is food, clothing, shelter, and a healthy feeling of superiority over our fellow mortals. Alas, probably true.

There are by my count four troubling horsemen that ride through the beginning writer's thoughts, offering motivation for his quest. There is writing to have written, which is to say writing to achieve fame. There is writing for sex and erotic ascendancy. There is writing for cash: no man but a blockhead, Dr. Johnson said, ever wrote but for money. And finally there is writing for revenge. Fame, sex, money, and revenge: this is the four-headed beast that faces the beginning writer. (It faces all writers, but over time most make some kind of peace with it.) Indulging one of these motives or another isn't necessarily fatal—revenge in particular can be a fiery, fertile muse. But all are dangerous. I'll talk about them in turn.

Some writers are motivated by the hunger for fame. They want to be known; they want to be recognized. When they walk down the street they want the cameras to click; when they enter a restaurant, they want to see cell phones raised high as though in a toast. They've never read Schopenhauer, or if they have they've ignored him. The dark sage says that a taste for fame is like a taste for seawater. A hit of recognition satisfies at first; maybe it ravishes. But quickly the satisfaction dissipates, and a compounded thirst cries out for more, more.

The most unlikely people want to write books—or to have written them. Movie stars need to tell the world their life stories or to put it on a diet. Politicians have at least a half dozen books in them, though it is almost always the same book. Spiritual teachers need to send their teachings abroad: even the admirable Dalai Lama gets about a book a year into circulation and though it is not always the same book per se, there are potent resemblances down the line. All sorts of human beings who are, I dare to speculate, not terribly prone to *read* books are gung ho to write and publish them.

And often—no secret here—these are books they never had to write, but only to have had written for them. The books are composed by people who are not quite people, writers who are not quite writers. They're written by ghostwriters, written by *ghosts*. The celebrity or the athlete or the politician almost never sits down with a pencil or hums up the computer and stares into a blank white rectangle. Instead the very important personage relaxes into a puffy black chair, pulls his sleeping mask over his eyes, and begins free-associating on his child-hood, his principles, or the dangers he's discerned in eating too much overprocessed wheat. The ghost records and jots notes and fires questions and tries to prime the rusty but elegant pump. Then the ghost writes draft upon draft, which the personage (who reads rarely) attempts to read. The personage likes the text not at all. It's time for round two, draft two. (Then three, then four.) That either the ghostwriter or the personage survives the ordeal is not unsurprising. But in time, the personage can say with a smile: "I have written. Here is my book."

I've often wondered about the term "ghostwriter." And now I think I understand it. The term is based on a reversal. For it is the personage who is the ghost: it is the personage who is too much of a cipher to sit down and organize his ideas and to render them in cogent prose. He's been leading a half life, a ghost's life—though society is prone to see it much differently. Society has given up on figuring out what the good life might be; society is interested in the enviable life the writer Adam Phillips observes. A certain sort of person does not pause to say, "Is this good or not?" Rather he asks (often subliminally) if this or that action, this or that acquisition, will prove to be enviable. Will it make my neighbors green? If yes, I must proceed. Writing a book and publishing it is, in many circles it seems, an element of leading the enviable life.

The personage who puts a book out has not actually composed it. And in some cases he may not really have read it either, or not all of it. (I once watched the former basketball star Charles Barkley listen with admiring interest as a fellow TV commentator told him what was in one of his books.) He hasn't composed it; maybe he hasn't even read it. But he has written.

There is still magic to the making of a book. The man or the woman who can do as much is still something of a Prospero. In the world, even in the current world, there are two kinds of people: there are those who have written and published a book and those who have not. The fact that people who do not read and aren't even prone to think much would want to join the ranks of book writers says something about the enduring allure of the book.

It's occurred to me too that people who cover themselves with tattoos—of whom there seem to be more all the time—are themselves aspiring writers, composing their autobiographies in hieroglyphics on the parchment of their skin. There one can find a record of their lives, assuming one knows how to read and interpret the signs, or that the tattooed personage is willing to be one's guide, which in my experience they're usually willing to do, often at exhaustive length. Here are records of past loves and deceased friends, tributes to family members and to athletes and prophets and superheroes who have somehow inspired the wearer. The tattooed personage has become a walking text. She doesn't just wear her heart on her sleeve, but her whole history and maybe her destiny across her entire body, which calls out to be read and understood—and then, with luck, accepted and loved.

It is a sad fact of the world: books that truly are books are written by writers. The books worth reading are books by people who have given their lives over to learning the art and the craft of composing. "The life so short the craft so long to learn," says Chaucer. He's talking about love, but he might as well be talking about writing. Almost no one turns aside from a distinguished career as a statesman and composes a brilliant treatise. Marcus Aurelius did it, but there have not been many such people in creation. Churchill received his Nobel Prize in Literature for tomes he at best partially wrote. John F. Kennedy found himself with a Pulitzer Prize for a book to which he made, at best, a minor contribution. But human beings wish to live *and* to write.

They want to be actors in the world. They want to be players. But then too they want the capacity to reflect and to turn their experience into melodious words. It happens, it happens—but not very often.

And the writer? Surely the writer would like to live. But from the time he throws himself into the game of making worlds with words, his actual life can become a secondary piece of business. At best, what others call his actual life is the sap that feeds the flower (if it is a flower) of his mind. He stops living and he begins observing. All that he sees exists first to stock his mind with images and metaphors and tales. I hoed beans to gather tropes, said Thoreau. A comely sight turns into a Henry Jamesian glimpse, food for a short story or a sketch. The writer doesn't always have what's called a life!

Hemingway grabbed the attention of the world because he appeared to solve the riddle. How could a writer have a *life*? He seemed to do it by being a man who was more than a man: hunting, fishing, drinking, brawling, marching through Africa in colonial state, getting married and married and married again. He became a figure of amazing allure: Papa, the Old Man of the Jungle; Papa, the Old Man of the Sea. Every man of the world could imagine being Hemingway; every writer could imagine himself being a man of action and man of thought, equally at home in the study and in the lion's seat at a legendary bar.

Maybe it happened: maybe Papa did manage to square the

circle. But Hemingway is Hemingway—and not many others have managed to pull off the feat.

The aspiration to be both author and full-fledged actor in the world may be a trap. But at the heart of the desire to have written lies something more than mere vanity. My friend wanted to be recognized at the party on the Upper East Side, to "Susan" Susan and to "Gore" Gore (as did many, come to think of it), but he probably wanted something more, too. It's something that the usually oblique poet Wallace Stevens evokes in a rather simple phrase. Stevens probably didn't feel he embodied this condition, though it was one he aspired to. He looked with admiration, he tells us, at "the man who has had the time to think enough."

Who is this person who has had time to think enough? This is the man (or, surely, the woman) who has taken the time to step out of the main road and to read and to ponder and finally (probably) to write. This is someone who has observed life carefully and on his own terms and drawn some conclusions. It's the sort of person that Emerson celebrates in "The American Scholar." It's a young person who has decided not to chase after early success. He's stepped aside from the throng and become a reader and a watcher. He's read carefully (and not in a slavish, overreceptive way), for as Emerson says, "There is then creative reading as well as a creative writing." He's developed for himself a sense of proportion: he knows that a popgun is only a popgun, even if the venerable of the earth say that it's the crack of doom. Then comes Emerson's great sentence: "In silence, in steadiness, in severe abstraction, let him hold by himself; add observation to observation, patient of neglect, patient of reproach; and bide his own time—happy enough, if he can satisfy himself alone, that this day he has seen something truly." He compounds his observations, this American scholar, and he collects his truths. And in time he knows: he knows who he is (as Socrates said he must) and he knows what the world is to boot.

Has anyone ever actually achieved this exalted state? If he has I have not met him face to face, though I've encountered a pretender or two, as most everyone has. But surely there are those with real claims to the distinction—human beings who have had the time to think enough. The divine Plato, as Coleridge liked to call him, may be one; Schopenhauer is another; and Emerson himself (provided you will sift and straighten him a bit) may make a third—or so I think. They found their truth and then made it manifest; their innermost became outermost, something Whitman too makes happen in *Song of Myself.* And the result of their efforts was a book, or a set of books. (Real books.)

I think many of us aspire to this kind of culmination and fulfillment. We want to have our say, let the world know our truth. But first of course we want to know it ourselves. The aspiration to have written is in most of its manifestations a silly one. "Hello Susan!" "Hi Gore!" But alongside the silliness rides a serious purpose. She who has written (and done it well) has figured it out. She's come to her own conclusions. Such a person possesses what we call character, in that any day we approach her on a matter of moment she is consistent and sure: she is always herself. And there is something true and admirable about this self, something that compels affection and respect even from the most wayward.

Imagine the person who has written and now finally needs to write no more! She's done her work; she's laid it down. And now she enjoys the view from the promontory, however high or low others take her particular vantage to be. A few writers nail it and then quit. William Blake stands out: he spent the last years of his life largely silent, his magnificent visionary poems all written and illustrated with engravings. He even began to get a bit of the recognition he deserved. He resolved his relations with his wife; his finances got more stable. On his deathbed he said that though he was weak in body, the entity he called the Real Man, or the Imagination, was as potent as it ever had been, maybe more so. He died a happy and fulfilled man.

Most writers don't make it there. When most of us talk about wanting to have written, what we mean is that what we'd like is to take a lifelong vacation, at full pay (or at what we imagine full pay ought to be). But there's another way to think about the state of having written as well: some, if only a very few, will be able to walk out of the game telling themselves that they truly have taken time to think enough and then to write it all down. To be one of them is no small matter; nor is it a small thing to aspire to be.

TO GET THE GIRL / TO GET
THE GUY

WHAT WRITER HAS not dreamed that writing could lead to a glorious erotic life? I'll get famous the writer says to himself. I'll become rich and well known and then I'll get the girl or the girls. I'll write a bestseller and then another one the novelist says, and men will lay treasures at my feet. I'll have my pick and I'll take my time choosing. Freud suggests that people write books for three reasons: fame, wealth, and love. They want to be loved in general: they want crowds to admire them and to cast envious looks their way. (They want the wages of having written.) But they also want to be loved specifically, up close and in a personal fashion, by this or that alluring individual.

And surely there have been writers who have been erotic champions. George Gordon, Lord Byron, was one. Byron was the original celebrity. After the publication of his first book-length poem, *Childe Harold's Pilgrimage*, Byron attained a fierce notoriety. "I awoke one morning," he said, "and found myself famous." He was already rich. Byron inherited an enormous fortune from his father's side of the family. And he was handsome as well. More than handsome really: men and women alike thought of him as beautiful. He had skin of alabaster, liquid brown eyes, auburn curls like sea spume, and a long white neck, like a swan's. The fact that he was rather short, inclined to put on weight, and had one clubbed foot apparently took nothing away from his erotic allure.

I awoke and found myself famous—and he was. Everyone, it seemed, wanted to go to bed with Lord Byron. He was much more seduced than he was seducing. Women got themselves rolled into carpets and smuggled into his rooms; they hid themselves in savory teak chests and popped out at propitious moments; they leapt into his coach and would not be pried loose—or so the legends tell us. He was besieged by men, too. Byron was bisexual it seems, and sometimes the male besiegers broke down the walls. He was especially prone to homosexual liaisons when he was traveling in the East and wrote about them in veiled—and not-so-veiled—form in the poetry, his letters, and his journals.

Byron could look something like an angel with his riot of curls and his upturned gaze—often seen because he tended to be shorter than his interlocutors. But he had a demonic side too, or at least he affected to have one. He was eventually branded "mad, bad, and dangerous to know." He probably committed incest with his half sister, Augusta Leigh, and he demanded that his wife perform what she considered unspeakable acts. Anne Isabella Milbanke, his wife, was a lady with a predilection for mathematics. Byron called her the "princess of parallelograms" and tormented her no end. Probably what he wanted was anal sex; it's not entirely clear. Whatever it was, she was not having any. Byron didn't seem to mind letting the world know about the more scandalous elements of his nature: he assumed, and rightly, that they made him more intriguing.

Or at least they did until word about incest with his half sister got around. It became advantageous then for Byron to leave London. He died of fever in Greece, where he went to aid in the Greek war of independence. He was in his later thirties—weary of life, and ready to leave it. One of his last poems is about the nearly insupportable pain of having turned thirty-six years old.

Byron's poetry is the kind of poetry that could make almost anyone fall in love. He's melodious, fluent, perfectly pitched, ironic, and, when he wants to be, quite funny. ("But O ye lords of ladies intellectual / Inform us truly, have they not henpecked you all?") He claimed to write best when he was on horseback moving at a steady canter, and he claimed almost never to have blotted and infrequently to have corrected a line. Whatever the truth of these statements, his poetry *sounds* like it broke perfectly into the world. For all its art, *Don Juan* has a richly conversational quality; it's as though you are being talked with (though never talked at) by the most spirited, charming, and worldly man in existence.

And—this is perhaps the most salient quality—the writing does not put any real demands on you. Once you've picked up Byron's idiom, it's all sailing on a glassy lake. Byron isn't out to change the world: if he has a moral purpose, it's to soundly spank those who are. He detests Wordsworth for being a pill, with his rabid nature worship; he thinks Coleridge is a raving obscurantist. (There's some sand grain of truth in this, though it's also true that Byron had little more ability to make or follow a philosophical argument than your pet Airedale.) Byron doesn't like people with big ideas or major theories or programs for universal reform. He idealizes nothing. If he grants integrity to anything in the world, it is first love—and for him and most of his rather worldly readers first love is clapped in the book of the past and locked away. Byron is a merry debunker. He skates over the surface of life; his verse skips like a stone. He defies gravity, in all senses of the word. When he felt as though he was growing heavy and ponderous and homely and old, he contrived to bring his life to an end, in the most romantic way available, fighting in what appeared to be a glorious and lost cause.

The contemporary writer who hopes to be an erotic force should no doubt study the life of Byron with care. He or she should consider that it doesn't hurt at all to start off both beautiful and rich. Those qualities may not be necessary, but surely they aren't beside the point either. After that, what should the erotically ambitious writer cultivate? A sense of ease probably. You'll never want to let them see you sweat, unless your particular form of perspiration results in a golden glow. Yeats's thoughts come to mind again here: "A line will take us hours maybe / Yet if it does not seem a moment's thought / Our stitching and unstitching has been naught." So even if you do labor hard to write, as Yeats did, or labor hard to be beautiful, as his two women friends in "Adam's Curse" purportedly do, you've got to hide it. The world loves a natural. Byron was one (it seems) and Yeats, a brutally hard worker, understood the allure.

The writer with an erotic goal tends to be a demonic angel, in something of the way Byron was. Noble as he may appear, he also carries a whiff of sin. He's been tapped on the shoulder by the devil's hand. An erotically alluring writer seems to be a fetching mix of innocence and experience, to borrow terms from Blake. He's the lamb and the lion in one. Any number of recent writers have tried this persona on: one thinks of my bow-tied friend's paragons, Gore Vidal, Susan Sontag, and of Bret Easton Ellis, Martin Amis, and even in his way David Foster Wallace.

But I think that the key element in being a writer with an erotic aura is the one that Byron understood so well. Don't put burdens on people. Don't ask them to be better than they are. Don't challenge their worldview and their habits. Don't even go far in subtly undermining their idiom by having the nerve to write in a different one. Norman Mailer said he hoped to effect a revolution in the consciousness of his time; that doesn't sort very well with the kind of clownish hijinks Mailer the celebrity writer had to perform in order to stay on the front page of the newspaper, or at least somewhere below the last entry in the gossip column. Mailer wanted to be significant and something like glamorous at the same time—good luck. To be sexy and a writer you've probably got to be light and you've got to be swift—and how well those qualities sort with genuine writing is an open question.

I'd daresay that genuine writing—the attempt to delight and instruct and to change the world or some quadrant or speck—is probably antithetical to erotic success and allure. I'd even say that the person writing makes you become doesn't have much chance to win and win in the erotic sweepstakes. This is in part because writers are often rather—well, scary. They may or may not have figured it all out; they may or may not have had time to think enough. But to other people who use their minds sparingly and almost exclusively to get what they want out of life, someone with a developed mind who thinks freely can be frightening. Such people talk in full sentences. Occasionally a complete paragraph emerges. Writers are deft with language. When they're off work it's still their running track and their jungle gym. These capacities are intimidating; these powers make other people self-conscious. They wonder, "Am I dumb?" They wonder, "Can I keep up?" Feeling dumb and feeling self-conscious are not states that go readily with feeling erotic attraction. "He's so sexy—he makes me feel stupid." This I daresay is a sentence that is never true. It may never have been uttered; it may be appearing here for the first time.

Writers are also prone to the deployment of irony. They may not know what irony is in any strict sense. No one may know what irony is. But they *sound* ironic nonetheless. There is, perceptibly, a double sense to what they say. They mean it and they don't mean it. To fall in love (or lust) people need to feel comfortable. They need to feel whole and at one with themselves—so they can get on with the business of becoming one with the person across the table. Irony is a duplicitous business: there is the overt sense, but then there is a secondary or subtle sense. But what the heck is it? This state of not knowing but guessing and speculating may have its pleasures, but it is probably not an erotic state.

One of Philip Roth's characters is trying to learn the art of seduction from an erotically successful friend. The friend lays it down. The average woman, the woman on the street, is not charmed by complex literary references; she does not rise to a quick flick of allusion to Melville. And she is not well disposed to irony, not at all. The woman on the street, the seducer says, hates nothing quite so much as she does irony.

The man on the street is not so well disposed either, especially when the ironist is a woman. It is no news to anyone, especially intelligent women, but men can become terrified of a woman who seems to know more, who clearly speaks better, and who maybe, just maybe scored higher on the SATs. Men like to be the boss in matters erotic. They like to primate around. They want to stand on the highest branch and holler. Anyone who interferes with this desire, though she may have to be tolerated, is unlikely to become a figure with shimmering erotic appeal. Byron who should have been the most secure of men erotically is himself afraid of those smart women: "Have they not henpecked you all?" (The implication being—they've pecked me more than a bit.) Maybe he married the Princess of Parallelograms with the intention of putting her and through her all thinking women in their places. It's hard to say.

Surely there are great poets who are also great lovers; they do often possess the gift of the gab and all that. But many of them fall more deeply in love with their verbs than with the panting virgin before them. They love the approach—the culmination much less, sometimes not at all.

Writers spend a great deal of their time alone and are in a certain sense always alone. They joy in the productions of their own minds and when it comes time to break out and connect with another person in the intimidating, arousing, confusing flesh and blood form, things do not always go well. And there is this, too. Writers can almost always *imagine* a lusher erotic paradise than any they might find or create in the actual (the merely actual) world. Too often they live in the land that Blake called Beulah, the world where all benign wishes come true, good things are got for nothing, and there are no contradictions.

Love—and erotic conquest—may also be bad for writing. (Though there are those writers—Shelley!—who cannot write without love.) We're told that history is written by the winners. Maybe. Surely literature is largely composed by and about the other constituency. We do not want to hear stories in which the protagonist moves effortlessly from strength to strength, conquering world upon world. At least we don't after the age of six or so. The story of the man who gets the girl or girls simply by wearing the right shirt, combing his hair just so, and showing up is not one that bears repeating. We may want to hear about victory from time to time, but it is the saga of defeat that draws one to read—and that is also the best subject for real writing. Writers are melancholy. They tend to silence, exile, and cunning—not empty noise, angling for invites, and the compounding of a solid game plan. Writers see the downside: when the sun's out they say it obscures their field of vision. To be a writer you may not have to exude death, the way Poe could do. But it helps to be, as Frost says he was, one "acquainted with the night."

I heard an interview with the guitarist from a band; it was called the Black Crowes I think. He said that for a while he wanted to be a writer so he could get girls. But then he noticed that all the writers he knew were guys whose teeth were going black because they couldn't afford the dentist, and who stuttered when girls walked into the room. I'd never heard of the Black Crowes, but I was assured they were huge. And the guitarist affirmed matters for me: the rock route worked just fine. He was a-swim in sex. So if sexual paradise is your game, you probably should turn off the laptop, turn on the guitar, and pen some lyrics. Keep them simple and keep them sincere. Let the love come through!

TO MAKE SOME MONEY

THERE IS LITTLE choice. When one decides to talk about writing and cash flow, it is virtually impossible not to begin with Dr. Johnson. His pronouncement on this matter has gathered renown. "No man," he famously said, "but a blockhead ever wrote except for money."

Johnson had a notoriously hard time getting his writing done even when money *was* involved. He said that whenever he attempted a poem (which wasn't terribly often) he would establish at the start how many lines he was going write. He would squeeze out a few. Then he would stop, chew his quill for a while, and begin counting how many lines were still left to be written. He may have spent as much time counting as he did composing. He was devoted also to working to the very tick of the deadline. When he wrote up the parliamentary debates of his day—debates he did not attend but that he had paraphrased for him by someone who had—the printer's boy was often left waiting at the door, while Johnson (now finally inspired) took up his work with a furor. Johnson was a great procrastinator, as great perhaps as Coleridge, and his muse was compounded of equal parts guilt and the need for pay.

For after a certain point in his life (and that point came rather early) Dr. Johnson lived off his pen. He was a denizen of what was then called Grub Street, though even from early on in his career he was a rather distinguished denizen. Eventually Johnson found himself rewarded with a royal pension and took no small pleasure in it—despite the fact he had maligned pension givers and pension takers in his famous dictionary.

Through most of his life Johnson wrote for money, didn't make much of it, and believed that only a fool would put himself through the grinding labors of composition for free. He tended to think that writing performed a service: some of it gave pleasure, some instructed, and some (the very best) did both. Johnson looked at his work as instructional. He taught people what they did not know. Or he reminded them of what they had forgotten, but should not have. "Men more frequently require to be reminded than informed," he said.

What did Johnson remind them of? He reminded them about their moral duty. His essays are about ethical behavior. He went on in his papers the *Rambler* and the *Idler* (the name of the latter must have been a cause of some unpleasantness to him) about the duties of husbands to wives, children to parents, rulers to ruled, and the ruled to the rulers. (Mostly he went on about the latter: Johnson was a royalist and a conservative.) Johnson strove to offer his readers material that was—a favorite word of his—"useful." When he thought about writing, he could readily compare what a writer did to what a table maker did. He said that he could freely criticize a craftsman who made him a faulty table, even though he himself could not make a table to save his life. The same was true of poetry. He might not be able to write it brilliantly himself, but as a reader—as a customer and consumer—he could very well criticize the product.

Johnson could stand in something like awe of the writers who gave you more than a mere product and who seemed actually to be inspired rather than workmanlike. He loved Pope; he revered Dryden; he disliked Milton's personality and his politics, but he read many passages of *Paradise Lost* with amazement (as anyone must). And he was amazed by Shakespeare—by his invention and variety and his capacity to draw "just representations of general nature." But Johnson largely saw himself as a craftsman, not an artist. People needed instruction—in manners, in morals, and in the appreciation of literature. Very well, Samuel Johnson gave it to them, or rather sold it to them, at so much per line. "No man but a blockhead ever wrote but for money."

Instructive writers write for money—and of course writers who give pleasure do, too. The men and women who write the books you see in the airport racks succeed when they are responsive to the needs of their customers. They do not sit at their desks thinking, "What will interest me to say today?" They think (on whatever level), "What does my reader, my customer, truly want to pay for and be diverted by?" The reader on the airplane does not want a work that tells him in the manner of the Apollo bust in the famous Rilke poem that he must change his life. No, he wants a book that will, say, take the anxiety that he feels as his plane hums down the runway toward takeoff and do something about it. He wants his anxiety turned into suspense. Hanging and hovering in blue and cloud-swamped space the prevailing question ought not to be: "What will happen to me?" The reader should be asking, "How will it go for Sam or Jose or for Esmerelda"—who has perhaps given in and slept with her new boyfriend a hundred pages too soon.

And are we not always hanging and hovering in some kind of at least slightly foreign space, the way we are in that airplane? "We hang in anxiety," Heidegger the philosopher of being says. By which he means, in part, that anxiety is always with us, or at least thrumming on the margins of our lives. Heidegger insists that living with anxiety was part of what we could do to make life "authentic." But many of us don't want to be authentic, at least in the philosopher's sense, at least not all the time. We would rather be calmed and if possible charmed—so we use a pill, a mantra, a drink, or a book. An effectively engaging story that doesn't challenge the reader at all delivers the equivalent of a half glass of wine's worth of buzz. Should a writer be paid for providing this service? Doesn't one owe the vintner and the waiter some quantity of coin? Only a blockhead would give his wine away for free. (Only a blockhead would write for nothing.)

Alcohol and writing, intoxication and reading—these subjects come together in a memorable poem by A. E. Housman called "Terence, This Is Stupid Stuff." Housman's friends have been taxing him for writing verse they find hard to stomach. It's too harsh, too bitter, far too pessimistic. The boys at the bar would like something much merrier. "Come," they tell him, "pipe a tune to dance to lad." Housman replies, telling them that the kind of poetry they want to hear is a form of intoxication—a way of getting to see the world as the world is not. Now Housman is not against getting drunk. "I have been to Ludlow fair," he says, "and left my necktie God knows where." He's apparently tied a few on—until "the world seemed none so bad, and I myself a sterling lad." Two drinks, it's said, will make a new man out of you. There's only one problem;

the new man wants a drink. And then the inevitable comes: "Down in lovely muck I've lain." And when Housman rises, "The world it was the old world yet: I was I, my things were wet." Housman says it's his business to write the kind of poetry that prepares you for a world in which there is "much good— but much less good than ill." And so he does.

Yet for stern medicine like Housman's not many people are willing to pay, and those who are often can't manage a high price. Housman is an accessible poet, but his pleasures are the harsh pleasures of contact with a stern principle of reality. He knows as much and is willing to accept the fact that he may never be the most popular of writers and that his work may not make him rich.

To write for money one must understand one's game. Housman writes for himself. He writes to express his own harsh view of the world: he wants to get it down as he sees it. If others want to partake of the vision or to learn from it, that's fine. But the writer who writes to make money puts his reader first—and he sees the reader in his day-to-day guise. He writes for the reader's self and not his soul. He gives the self a vacation from the real and transports him to a lotusland of one sort or another. Or he gives the reader practical advice that will help him buy the right stocks, eat the right food, vote for the correct party, seed his garden, or repair his perforated roof. He gives him the inside story about how the world works: Why did the market crater? Why did the Soviet Union collapse? How did the war start and why did it end? Such subjects the writer who serves his reader may cover and expect to be paid for.

But there are some writers for whom the subtitle of the book is always "The Way It Is for Me." They write to explore the lairs of their thoughts, they write to deploy and maybe to enlarge their imaginations, and they write to find out who and what they are. They ask for readers who will share—or at least entertain—their sense of things, in all its complexity and (usually) its harshness. And then—sometimes—not quite knowing themselves, they put out their right hand, palm up, and wait for the world to drop its coin. Often they wait for a long time. Writers who write to change the world go begging. The world does not want to be told to change itself—and if it tolerates the insult to its ongoing state, it surely will not willingly pay much of a price to be so insulted.

A sadness at the heart of writing! Serious writers constantly expect the treasure to fall in their laps for the strong medicine they dispense. They do not see why their higher, more serious work should not be rewarded.

A sketch cartoon I saw (or imagined) once: an artist wearing a beret and puffing a Gauloises stands at his easel contemplating a half-completed drawing of a plutocrat in top hat and tie. Beneath the sketch the words: BOURGEOIS HOG. Standing askance by the easel is the very man, the plutocrat (or hog). The artist stares expectantly at his model and says, "Could you give me a grant to finish my artwork?"

A sadness of writing! Writers who mean to give practical instruction or easy pleasure want to be acknowledged as artists. They want to be spoken of in the same breath as world-changing poets and sublime novelists. Virginia Woolf and Stephen King on the same stage, on the same Parnassus, in the same sentence. In our culture at least they have largely succeeded. The pulp fictionists appear with the high-minded poets. They cop some of the same awards, are washed in the same limelight. But on some level, the pulpists must feel themselves to be frauds. They have bought their way into the game—for they support their publishing houses, support other poorer writers (or so we are told). The entertainers must know the medals they wear are not theirs. They skipped the true campaign, never went under fire, never heard a bullet whiz up close. They are like those Soviet generals who are covered with decorations but have never been brave.

This is not to say that those who write for money don't have powers of their own—and humanly useful powers, too. I recall once sitting in a restaurant in my town when one of the most successful authors—successful in monetary terms—walked through the door. It was John Grisham wearing a bespoke suit of what appeared to be linen—with his beautiful wife, with his kindly manner, with his easy Southern confidence. Grisham writes a book a year. He spends six months writing, and then he spends six months enjoying the manifold fruits of his labors—or so the story goes. He does not claim to be Shakespeare or even Dickens, but someone who can give you an enjoyable hour's reading before nodding off or before your train arrives.

At our table one of my colleagues—we were all English profs—looked up as Grisham made his entrance and said, "John Grisham, the novelist. Sold a lot of books." A pause, a moment for reflection, and then with the best will in the world, my friend said, "We could all do that if we wanted to. We could all write that sort of book." There was nothing harsh or resentful in my friend's voice. He's not that sort of guy. But I have to confess he pushed me into mild shock.

We could all write that sort of book—that sells a half-million copies? We could all write turn-the-page, turn-the-page until a mild sort of windstorm rises from the scene sort of book? We're literate and even literary: we've read a lot (more than Grisham, I'd bet), and if need be we could do the job.

Really! Really? Because from my point of view there is no chance that any of us could have. It's hard to write for money and succeed—hard to create plots and characters that are just the right fit with the audience's need for diversion. It's tough to put the language at the right level—those lines of clichés that are not quite clichés, words that have been used often together (so as to be familiar) but not so often as to really bore the reader. Such books are hard to write. If there has ever been a writer who could go from writing for himself and expressing the world as he sees it, and doing it well, to writing popular books for money, I have never encountered him or her. That person may not exist.

Schopenhauer said that the moment you write for money or even accept a dime for your work, you are going to compromise it. You stop writing the truth as you see it (or the truth proper) and begin to write what your audience, in its most banal and commonplace guise, wants to read. To the commercial writer, money is the measure of success. To earn well is to write well; to write well is to earn well. To the more serious writer, every nickel earned with the pen should make him question whether his work is genuine. Even a readership that is too large, or not the right quality, should give him pause. Most men and women cannot bear all that much reality—and reality in concentrated and often harsh form is what the authentic writer frequently delivers. Or so at least says the noble Schopenhauer, lord of all pessimists past and to come, and also a true lord of philosophy.

Socrates knew that money and the truth did not sort well with each other. He took no cash for his teachings and castigated his enemies, the Sophists, for their money hunger. Socrates knew the score—the writer in search of hard truths cannot expect money—or much love either. (For that he should join a rock band.) No accident that the people of Athens rose up and condemned Socrates to death for disturbing their mental peace. Schopenhauer says that the young man who has studied and prepared and thought, thought, thought will break into the world with his book expecting fame, wealth, and the love of beautiful women. What he'll get is irritation and maybe anger. He'll be lucky, Schopenhauer says, to escape with his skin. As to his hopes for cash—those are hopes in vain.

TO GET EVEN

PEOPLE WRITE TO get even with others; they write to get
even with the world. There's not much doubt about it; they
do. The desire for revenge—along with the desires for fame
and wealth and erotic satisfaction—are the four most alluring
(and potentially destructive) motives for writing. It's been said
that writing proceeds from a narcissistic wound. (Edmund
Wilson and Harold Bloom say it, albeit in their different ways.)
Someone or something gores the writer's sense of who he is and
what he deserves and he takes up his pencil (or puts fingers to
keys) to settle the score. Who ever feels that he gets what he
deserves? Who ever feels that the world loves him enough?
Who truly believes that all of his virtues have been perceived
and rewarded to the right measure? We all, at least at times, are
creatures of injured merit.

How does the writer get even? A thousand different ways!
The most common way, perhaps, is through fiction. He relives
his family life in his imagination and he gets the chance to call
it as he sees it. All of the culprits are there: feckless mother,
monster father, the siblings who crushed the tender author's

tender sensibility—or tried. (Freud tells us that when we dream of flourishing insects we are probably dreaming of brothers and sisters.) They are all disguised thinly enough. How many people have gotten the gift of red hair or a large nose through the generous bequest of the family author?

Writing to get even is sometimes the specialty of the youngest child in the family. The youngest is the fairy-tale child. She's the one who under other circumstances might be rambling into the world to traverse the enchanted forest, slay the fiery dragon, dig up the pot of gold, and save the kingdom. But in actual life she may have felt herself to be Cinderella before the Prince came—and the Prince never really did come. She was squashed by the mean sisters and banged around like a paddleball by the nasty older brothers. So it's time to get even. It's time to get square.

I know of a writer who made a great success of a first novel based on her family. The little girl in the corner had apparently been storing up a record of all the familial insults like an angry accountant. She published her book. It sold. And naturally some of the kids in the family felt they had been tossed and gored unfairly. Brothers and sisters drank toasts in blood to her come-uppance. Reconciliations came slowly if they came at all. One of the kids, a girl, responded more vehemently. Word was that she left her job and entered a creative writing program (at rather large expense) at a well-reputed university. The objective? "To write a family novel that features a neurotic younger sister who never washed her greasy hair." I hear she wrote it and got it published, too.

Revenge can be a powerful muse. At a certain point in his career, Philip Roth found himself divorced from his wife, the actress Claire Bloom. Not long after the divorce was final,

Bloom stepped forth with a book about life with Philip Roth. She had not cared for that life much at all. He was selfish and cheap and philandering, controlling and cruel. Roth got to read this himself and then, no doubt, he got to discuss it with his friends, or remaining friends. What did he do?

The blow of the Claire Bloom book—a bit of revenge in its own right—might readily have knocked him off and out of writing for good. It's not all that commonly mentioned, but writers expire all the time. They perish as writers, but maybe they perish a bit as humans, too. Keats was said to perish from a bitter review—a piece of nonsense if taken literally, but not without significance as a metaphor for the life and death of certain artists. To write poetry on the highest level (or even on the rather modest level of Keats's early volume) requires a degree of sensitivity. One must be responsive to the more subtly turning nuances of language and of life. But that sensitivity also inclines one to be readily hurt by reviewers with their poison-tipped darts. For surely no one is more likely to write out of the spirit of revenge—the desire to get even—than the book reviewer.

Book reviewers pretend to review the volume, but one knows that the volume is always the man or the woman. He who touches this book, touches a man, Whitman says. Claire Bloom did more than review the book that was Roth— or the books. She reviewed the Roth that was Roth and found him bitterly wanting. Roth might well have wound himself into a twisted shape and inched back inside a conch shell. But he didn't.

He answered back with a volume called *I Married a Communist*. In it, Claire Bloom becomes Eve Frame. Her daughter Anna—who seems to have sowed rich discord in the house—becomes an unlovable being named Sylphid. Roth is relatively gentle with Eve/Claire, but with Sylphid/Anna, not terribly. It seems he may have gotten just the right amount of revenge in the novel. And though it's far from his best, it did probably serve to discharge his spleen and let him move on to other work. A little revenge—a little but not too much.

Still, it's clear that throughout the book Roth is not only enacting a certain measured revenge, but also contemplating it. One character says, "Revenge[:] nothing so big in people and nothing so small, nothing so audaciously creative in even the most ordinary as the workings of revenge. And nothing so ruthlessly creative in even the most refined of the refined as the workings of betrayal."

On came *The Human Stain*, *The Plot Against America*, *Exit Ghost*, *The Dying Animal*, and a string of splendid late-career books. The work poured forth in a shimmering profusion. He was doing strong work late into life—and it is hard to imagine that the books were not an act of revenge, or a vengeful anti-revenge to the Claire Bloom book. His ex-wife may have imagined he would respond with an overt and appalling counterblast, maligning her and at the same time firing her career. He went back into his writing studio and toiled away and created—as a revenge that wasn't one—the sort of book that showed the world that what his ex-wife had had to say about him did not matter much at all. And as to Claire Bloom, maybe her book was a balm to her as well. In time she appeared in the film *The King's Speech*, playing the Queen of England.

Saul Bellow, slightly older than Roth, had a taste for literary feuds. He seems to have been on the border of one with Roth himself. Addressing the prowess of his younger competitor he simply said, "What hath Roth got?" (Plenty it turned out.)

Bellow sometimes seemed to love a literary feud above almost all other things; he got into one with William Phillips, the rather prosaic second banana at *Partisan Review*. He thought Philips was a long-winded bore. "One of the nice things about *Hamlet*," Bellow said, thinking of his antagonist, "is that Polonius is stabbed."

The urge for revenge can act as a muse for some writers. It apparently did for Bellow in what some think is his best book, *Herzog*. Herzog, the title character, more or less stands in for Bellow. He is a well-intentioned, radically unworldly, erotically avid professor of intellectual history. While he's up in the Berkshires with his wife, straining to finish his book, his life falls apart. He can't get his writing done, he can barely read, he can't think straight. His wife, Madeleine, has fallen into an affair with his best friend, Valentine Gersbach, and Herzog/Bellow is destroyed by it.

It happened that way in life—or some version of it did. But the man who stole Bellow's wife away was not a radio personality in Pittsfield, but a SUNY English professor named Jack Ludwig. Even now, one runs into Ludwig endorsers who thought he got a terribly raw deal in Bellow's depiction of him. And of course Ludwig wrote a novel of his own answering back to Bellow. It's called *Above Ground*.

But debts must be paid—at least for certain writers. To these writers, the art of writing is the art of combat. They model their careers on the careers of boxers and generals—though they are not always willing to say as much. They believe on some level that writing is a test of virility and manliness. (Hemingway may have taught them as much.) They are like boxers in the ring. When someone catches them with a shot, as Jack Ludwig did Bellow, they have to repay. They can't let an insult pass. They lie in wait to rap the guy who gave them that scorcher of a review all those years ago. When Mailer first met John Leonard, Leonard was a pup, reasonably new to literary New York, and Mailer was busy being Mailer, king of Manhattan. The encounter went like this, give or take: "I greatly admire your work," Leonard said to the great man. And then: "What are you working on now?" Mailer went into his Texas accent, usually not a comforting sign: "Well, Leonard, I'm doing a new collection of poems, since I know how much you admire my poetry." Leonard didn't quite know what Norman was getting at. Then he remembered. He had reviewed a volume of Mailer's verse five or six years earlier on his radio show in Berkeley, California, and he had not been pleased with Mailer's effort, not at all. Mailer tracked all his reviews and he remembered them. Mailer kept score.

You have to keep the ego in shape. You have to exercise it and give it the diet it needs—maybe sex, maybe money, and maybe revenge, too. And then it will repay you with endless creative juice. Or so some writers think. You have to be like Achilles, an Achilles of literature. Never let an insult pass; never take a tap on the chin you do not requite.

Even a writer as benevolent overall as George Orwell owned to a having a vindictive streak. In "Why I Write," he admitted that one of his motives was to get back at the schoolteachers and bosses who had thought too little of him, or thrust him aside. The settling of scores! In "Such, Such Were the Joys," Orwell takes aim and fires at the grotesque crew who caned him and tormented him at an English public school. It's a splendid essay—and a model for my own writing about education, for what it's worth. Would it have existed without the spirit of revenge?

Then there is book reviewing. To hear some writers tell it, the most vindictive people in the world are book reviewers. But they are not paying back this insult or that. It is nothing so specific. No, the angry book reviewer's gripe is more existential. They have a gripe with the world and with nature. Their gripe is with their own talent or lack thereof. They are enraged at having been left out in the disposition of true gifts and wish to puncture every man or woman who has been endowed. They damn with faint praise; they damn with loud imprecation. They love to take down the best and see them squirm in the dust. They show their fair-mindedness by picking out undistinguished books by undistinguished authors and sending up hecatombs to them. They love to "discover" new and meretricious talent and denounce the old and the true. Or it's the reverse.

Recently, serious writers will tell you, book reviewers have adopted another tactic in their ongoing war against creation. The book reviewers have decided to review crime stories, romance, and potboilers full of eye of newt and toe of frog and worse. And, serious reviewers that they are, they review those books in the tone of high seriousness—or at least as seriously as they review aspirants to the true laurels. Do they ever mention that reading Stephen King is a rank waste of time? Not at all. They aim to reflect taste and not to elevate it. They echo vox populi and praise the easy pleasures of the crowd. And what is this but a long-term strategy of aggression against true talent? What is it but a form of revenge? (Why be a writer if you can't be hyperbolic from time to time?)

Writers sometimes fight back. Martin Amis seems to be the progenitor of a telling line against the book reviewers. When I get a crummy review, he's said, then I pause and I ask myself: Is that really what reviewer X wanted to be when he grew up? A book reviewer? Is that really what he hoped and dreamed? True enough, maybe. Kids want to be knights and sages and sometimes even damsels in and out of distress. Some will tell you they want to be writers. But no kid will ever say he wants to be a book reviewer. Hold fast to the dreams of your youth, said Schiller.

The reviewers: perhaps they are the most prominent of writers who compose out of a spirit of revenge. But serious writers sometimes do that, too. Revenge can be a bitter muse, but sometimes it's an effective one. So much of what the great essayist Hazlitt composed seems to come out of the spirit of injured merit. He was a failure in love—and he writes for vindication against the simple (but complex) girl who dumped him. He made himself ridiculous among the literary avant-garde of his day, chiefly Coleridge and Wordsworth. Both of them he assaulted bitterly and often on a personal level. (Yet his perceptions about their poetry are so telling that the essays live on, as Hazlitt surely hoped.) At one point he launches a fierce attack on Coleridge's nose, which he sees as pathetically small and undistinguished. And the nose, says Hazlitt, is "the rudder of the face, the index of the will." STC's is "nothing—like what he has done."

The nasty reviewers and the whole unpleasant establishment can be a goad—maybe even an inspiration. Pay them back! Harold Bloom, whose work has transcended the genre of literary criticism, cried out once in print about being reviewed in the "weakest" possible way by legions of academic detractors. But he confessed that it was all to the good. They were, he said, getting my work done for me. He was writing to show 'em and to show 'em up.

Everyone knows that the literary feud—the tit-for-tat sweepstakes—is the mainstay of a certain kind of writer. Think of Vidal and Mailer, Mailer and Buckley, Hellman and McCarthy, Naipaul and Theroux. Writing is hard. It's tough to get up in the morning and look at the white snowfield of a trackless page. How to push forward? Use anger; use rage if you have to. Settle scores. And if you have no scores to settle, then create a few for yourself, not only for the purposes of public relations, but also for the purposes of inspiration. Hot-blooded, hot-tempered, always ready to take offense: the writer as duelist. Pace off twenty yards and then turn, word processors blazing. Anger can produce eloquence. That much anyone who has ever been in a spousal tiff knows. Rage is inspiration. But what it inspires—that's another question.

For the dangers of writing for revenge are manifold. How easily the vengeful writer loses distance and irony. How quickly he exposes the smallest version of himself. Despite its marvelous prose, the undersong of *Herzog* is too often a protracted masculine whine. Oh those women! Oh the false friend! Looking back at an exchange with Mailer that became physical, Vidal called it "the night of the small fists." He was embarrassed by it all and so in time was Mailer. It brought them both some attention, but lowered the esteem and expectations with which people approached their work. Even Dante, grand as he is, suffers from his vindictiveness. He settles too many scores when he populates hell and purgatory. He undermines his sense of proportion when he places his petty contemporaries in the pit beside figures from myth and legend. Dante even installs two figures in hell— Fra Alberigo and Branca Dora (traitors to guests)—who are not dead at the time he is writing the *Commedia*, so hungry is the master for retribution. Yet still, the poem will live eternally.

Writing for revenge may not be as dangerous as writing for money or fame or love. It can get you moving in the morning, give you a jolt. But in the end the purer and more detached spirit, the spirit of a Tolstoy, who writes to elevate mankind, is the one most likely to prevail.

In pragmatic America, results are everything. That you get where you want to go is what matters—so long as you don't break the law or get caught doing it. Success is all. In the East, matters tend to be different. The Buddha cares far more for intention than he does for result. If you do things for the right reasons, you will emerge with a benevolent smile, even if the results appear to be stamped by failure.

On the matter of writing, I think it best to listen to the wisdom of the Pali texts: intention matters. There are good intentions and bad and some that abide in shades of gray. The beginning writer ought to ponder the issue.

TO STRENGTHEN THE MIND

THE MIND IS a muscle. The people who say so most often—football coaches and geometry teachers and the like—aren't always the most sage. But that doesn't mean there isn't truth in the idea. The mind's a muscle and writing can make it strong. Writing can mess you up, too—no doubt about that. It can send you deeper into desire for cash and fame and no-point sex and revenge. But it can do some fine things for you, too. It's time to focus on some of those.

In order to write, you have to think. You have to take what's in your head and put it into coherent sentences: there needs to be a subject and a verb. Adjectives often help (though not too many, we're told). One sentence has to follow from the next, not like boxcars on a train. That's too strict, too predictable. But one has to be in strolling distance from the next. In her journal, Susan Sontag asks herself when she can claim that she's truly and actually thinking. She has to admit it. Only when I'm writing, she says. Or when I'm in conversation with someone I like (or love) and respect. (Plato's dialogues are built on such a premise.) But the rest of the time?

Sontag's mind was alive and alert and large enough, and she was interested in almost everything. (She once described herself as having ASD—attention surplus disorder.) But Sontag would admit it: not writing, not talking, the best that she or most of the rest of us could hope to produce is what William James described perhaps too kindly as stream of consciousness. Along it goes burbling and babbling and looping back on itself. It's not a pure stream, this stream of consciousness. It contains all sorts of figments and trifles, old memories, partially atrophied grudges, semiplausible hopes, and, not the least, fantasies, dreams, aspirations, and frustrations of a sexual sort. And the stream seems to flow where it likes. It lazes from one topic to another, and then simply slows down, pools up, and becomes gummy swamp.

Sometimes this is fine. A writer, as García Márquez says, must know how to relax. But the stagnant pool and the brook that babbles something close to nonsense—those are not the mind's ideal. When a fine writer is composing, when a splendid talker is holding forth, when a rich conversation is in gear, an almost athletic beauty and grace come into play. "How noble in reason" we can be, Hamlet says. And it is true. Yet given the chance, most of us will let the mind lie fallow for days on end.

We use it when we need to use it, which is to say we use our minds to advance our causes in the world. We plot to fill our desires; we scheme to get what we want (and usually, as Mick and Keith tell us, end up at best with what we need). We play chess with life. We try to push forward our pawns, protect the king, develop bishops and rooks, with the idea of winning this or that practical victory. We want a new job/house/car/lover. And there is satisfaction in deploying the strategizing mind. It can be a pleasure to get the best price or even from time to time to ride free. There is a practical statesman, a Ben Franklin type, dwelling inside each of us.

But we want more than a mind that's a stream of consciousness or a sloshing swamp; and we want more than a mind that functions as a consigliere, a shrewd adviser that merely helps advance our desires. We want the mind to be free to capture what is true and beautiful, at least from time to time. We want to look for truths that are going to last and don't apply to ourselves and ourselves alone. (Or we want to have the freedom to debunk what passes now for general truth.) And in this sort of quest, writing and conversation of the best sort are crucial. We may discover truth and we may disclose beauty. Or we may not. But the effort to do so strengthens the mind in manifold ways.

For the mind is more like a muscle than we think. The body of the athlete grows strong and effective under intense workouts and a salubrious diet. Where there was flab and ungainly motion, there is soon (or at least eventually) a beautiful tautness and fluidity. We can change our bodies; many people do. It is a hard fight, but a worthy one.

A man I know of had inflated himself up close to three hundred pounds. He was on the border of having diabetes. His feet hurt, his back hurt, he couldn't move without a groan, and he was barely forty years old. He'd been an athlete when he was young and one day, out of shame maybe, he resolved to get back in shape. He had young children; he had fresh responsibilities. It seemed bad form to go off and die on them anytime soon.

He started with a cymbal-clashing fall. He went out to the beach the first day and ran three miles. The next morning he could not rise from bed under his own power. When he did get up eventually, with help, a step forward brought him near tears. He had never been so sore. He slept almost all day and through the next night. But the following morning, he went back to the beach. He walked a quarter of a mile one way and a quarter mile back home. He felt horrible. But he went back and back and he never missed a day. He stopped choosing his diet from the donut-related food groups. He stopped emptying cans of beer, though he did dispatch a glass of wine from time to time. This went on for six months, then a year. He did a little more and he did it a little better every day. At the end of that time, he was not himself anymore. He'd lost seventy pounds and become reacquainted with his feet. He was another person, with a different body. That body wasn't going to live forever, but major bus accident withstanding, he was not going to die tomorrow. He had been reborn the only way non-churchly people acknowledge you can—by hard labor (which also, he testified, gave him some potent satisfaction). He had made himself a new body. Granted he had needed to use the old one for raw material and the old one was forty years old with some wear on the major parts.

The case for writing is not unrelated. It can give you a new mind. I don't want to overpromise here. Like our friend's body this new mind will use the mind you possess as its basis and it can't go worlds beyond. But you might be surprised.

For in many ways, writing is to the body what exercise is to the mind. Given sufficient provocation, or lack of it, the mind seems to want what the body wants—to regress to a vegetable state before its time. We have a tendency to inertia, both physical and mental. It is possible that in the people who appear to be most energetic that tendency is strongest. Said Macaulay of Dr. Johnson: he had a "morbid propensity to sloth and procrastination." But he also wrote a dictionary by himself. Though there was a gang of boys that swarmed around him like monkeys, running off to look matters up occasionally, it was mostly Sam Johnson of Lichfield who did the job. France had needed the entire French Academy to do it for them. England needed one fellow, the indolent Dr. Johnson.

If Johnson had had television, we might not have the dictionary, or the *Lives of the English Poets* either. For TV is a double-barreled precipitator of indolence, stalling out the mind and rendering the body recumbent. But in my experience, radical indolence of mind and body are often a sign of considerable energy that has been pent up for some reason or another. The answer: push forward. Push forward: preparatory of course to protracted rest and reward. Potentially energetic people often grow lazy because they believe that there is really nothing worth doing. Writing can wake up somnolent energies. Writing is something worth doing.

Writing can take the sloppy stream of consciousness and give it form and purpose. Writing takes what is vague and empty and slothful in our thoughts and gives it shape, so we can examine it and pass a verdict on whether it ought to stand or not. When we write, we *make sense*. The common phrase reveals something: sense will not make itself. Sense is a rather uncommon commodity. A coherent argument or an organic spectrum of images is the exception, not the rule.

It is an affront to all proponents of radical democracy and the solidarity of men and women the world over, but it is nonetheless true: most human beings do not think very much. Many are like the primitive countryman in Frost's "Mending Wall." When his neighbor asks him why there needs to be a wall between their two properties—will the apple trees on one side ever trespass and eat the fallen pinecones on the other?—his neighbor does not really think when he replies. He reverts to his father's saying: Good fences make good neighbors. And as Frost's narrator (whose own thinking has some flaws) says, it was his father's saying and he likes having remembered it so well. I find it surprising how many members of the purportedly thinking classes such as teachers and pundits seem hardly to think at all. While many carpenters and masons and waitresses have minds constantly abuzz.

When we don't offer slogans, we often produce something on the verge of mere jumble. I'm glad that in *Ulysses*, James Joyce took the time to chronicle an average man's average thoughts on an average day. But love Joyce as I do, after a few pages of it, I know why I usually want to read the thoughts of people who have passed beyond the average, and read them on their best days, for there is little time remaining to us, no matter how much we happen to have.

The mind can expand. This is Plato's point in *The Republic*. When a student walks out from the cave of shadows into the region of the sun and moon—the region of true knowing—it hurts. His eyes blink from the light; his head pulses from the strain. He feels wearied after too much exertion, much as the athlete does. It takes time to make himself worthy of his new destiny—becoming a thinker. But that is, in truth, simply to become a human being, for a human being is a rational animal to Plato, and some of us who go on two legs (some of us feather-less bipeds) alas do not quite qualify. Thinking makes one a man or a woman. Plato seems to have followed Socrates in the *doctrine* that conversation is at the heart of thought. But then too Plato, against the dictates of his teacher, wrote and wrote and wrote. Make up your mind, we say. What is writing if not the best way to do precisely that? Make up your mind!

Diet and exercise, says the athlete. If writing is the mind's exercise, then reading is its diet. As a teacher I can attest to a distressing fact. There are many young people now, some with real promise, who are interested in becoming writers. They love to write. They compose and compose until the computer keys are in danger of wearing out. But many of them do not really read. Oh, they read for pleasure: dull science fiction, fantasy, and adventure. But they do not want to read books that are the caliber of the books they hope to write. Writing is reading; reading is writing. Hemingway, the figure who did the most to masculinize writing this past century, trying to pass it off as a cousin of hunting and warfare, freely confessed that he read for hours a day.

By reading you learn how it's done. You keep your standards high. And constantly, constantly, you get fresh ideas. Books are your diet when you are a writer and if what you consume are the candy and carbohydrates of the literary world, then you will probably produce nothing better, no matter how hard you work. Books need to be meat and vegetables, strong greens, ripe fruits. Is it possible to be a writer in America and never to have dropped all the way into Melville or Dickinson, the prophet Whitman, or Emerson, the sage of Concord, Massachusetts?

Emerson may have told us that genius is always the enemy of genius through overinfluence, but one deals with that through struggling with the great and making one's way both with and against them. To ignore them is to ignore the sun and the stars. The best books create the best writing—or at least the best writing one is capable of doing. The best diet helps make the best runner or rower. How many writers' work has declined over time in part because, without quite knowing it, they now subsist on a diet of literary junk food? They spend too much time at the movies. They watch a lot of TV.

Writing can also lend itself to the re-creation of character— dare one say even the improvement of character. I once heard Bernard Malamud say that he thought revision was one of the most dignified and ennobling pursuits a person could take up. By all accounts Malamud, who taught at Bennington College when I was a student there, revised fiercely. He was not a natural, though he wrote a fine novel about a man—a ballplayer—who was. He went over and over and over his work. He brought his sentences to perfection or as close to perfection as he could. And this he felt to be character building.

He was right. Going back and back and back at a project is based on a fundamental perception. Nothing is ever quite right; nothing is ever good enough. In revision the writer admits to mortality and the flaw that's at the center of being human—or at least he does if he revises with the intensity that Malamud apparently brought to the game. He deploys and he develops what may be the human characteristic most important for success in any endeavor: persistence. For everything must be worked on. Rarely does one get it quite right the first time. In a marriage, in a career, in the rearing of children, failure is the order of the day. It doesn't work right; it doesn't play correctly— whatever it is. So what is to be done? Hit it one more time. Pull your energies together and give it another shot. One could even say that character at its best is the capacity to acknowledge you are wrong, or at least that matters could be better, and then throw yourself into repair. The house is always breaking down, disorder is everyplace, and there is no carpenter or fix-it guy to call except oneself.

If we can revise a text, maybe we can revise our characters—and do so in the writer's way of making things a little bit better, one step at a time. We can bring the same hard eye to our own affairs that we bring to the words that dance (or should dance) before us on the page. Make no mistake. An essay has a spirit. Novels and short stories do, too. Maybe a text is the closest analogue to a human spirit that we have. "This is no book," says Whitman. "Who touches this, touches a man." (It is a line that I cannot get away from or do without.) The text is a self, the self a text. It is not easy to improve one or the other. But it can be done.

To revise well we have to begin by detaching ourselves. Usually we're dug deep inside the trench of self. We hide behind the earthworks; we don't want to hear a negative word, much less pronounce one about ourselves. The beginning writer quails at the first piece of disinterested criticism he receives. For he knows it is he himself being criticized; that text *is* his spirit. But in time he learns to listen bravely and to take to heart what he needs.

The critic David Bromwich says that one of the most important powers one acquires in becoming an academic is the power to listen to what you do not want to hear about your work. Graduate school in the humanities cultivates many abilities. But one of the chief ones is the capacity to sit down and shut up and listen while someone with more experience tells you how you can improve. I once asked a teacher of mine, the formidable medievalist and poet Marie Borroff, where I was weakest as a scholar and writer. I can still recount what she said, pretty much word for word. It was a hearty dish, served without sugar, and it's stood me well for a long time. One does not have to attend an academy to get this kind of nutrition. There are many sources to be found.

How do you know that a criticism made by another or your-self is valid? How do you recognize criticism that can help you to grow? It is impossible to have absolute knowledge here. But I would say that when you hear sharp words from someone, either about yourself or your work, and they sting a little, something may be up. And if you find that you cannot, however hard you try, forget those words, well then, the truth does sometimes taste a bit like salt. You've been found out by another or by yourself: time to reconsider, improve, fix—time to make it new.

TO GROW

I T'S HARD TO remember everything one learned in graduate school. There are times it is hard to remember anything at all. This is so even when one has had the best teachers, which I feel I did. But at least one moment in a seminar on Shelley and Keats, taught by the wonderful scholar and critic Geoffrey Hartman, has stayed with me. It taught me something about both writing and the reasons for writing that might be arguable, but mean no less to me for that. Writing and reading can strengthen the mind the way exercise and eating right can strengthen the body. But I think writing can contribute to the growth of what I'd like to call the spirit, too.

You have to understand, Professor Hartman said, something central about John Keats. (Keats is a hero of this book, as is no doubt becoming plain.) He wants each one of his individual poems to count. He wants you to be absorbed and maybe even moved. But he wants something else as well. The poem matters to him, but what matters as much—maybe matters more—is the poem that it puts him in a position to write next.

Keats's poems, in other words, are dedicated to the growth of his spirit. He is always trying to put himself in a position to surpass himself. With every consequential poem, he is attempting to grow. He wants to get himself in a place where he can write another better poem. He wants to expand his spirit and then be able to expand it further.

The process isn't only about poetry. Keats didn't just want to become a better poet. Though he certainly did want that: he died with the belief that though his career was short he would be "among the English poets." And so he is.

But Keats also seems to have believed that expanding his capacities as a poet would entail expanding his capacities as a human being. He wanted, as Hartman put it—using the sort of avian metaphor that the romantics themselves were prone to—to "molt into a higher humanity." True or not for Keats—I think it is—people do write in order to grow. They write so as to make themselves better men and women. They write to engage in *Bildung*, or self-shaping. They write to enlarge their minds and increase the reach of their hearts. Keats writes about this process in an amazing letter in which he describes the poet's progression through phases. The poet begins in the infant or thoughtless chamber where all is mystery; and then there is the chamber of maiden thought, where the beginning poet (the young woman or young man) begins to test the world. Then there's the next chamber, which is the one that Keats believes that he is stepping into as he writes. The chamber of maiden thought is full of beauty and wonder. Its inhabitant lives there in delight. There is nature, there are books, there are friendships (Keats was a wonderful friend), and there is often the beginning of love.

But to grow as a poet (which is perhaps to grow as a human being), you cannot stay in the chamber of maiden thought forever, singing the songs of spring. You have to step away from this world of earthly delights and feel what Keats (borrowing from Wordsworth) calls "the burden of the mystery." In the next chamber we see that the world is full of sorrows and miseries. We understand that life everywhere is infected with pain. In the great nightingale ode, Keats talks about the mortal land where "palsy shakes a few sad last grey hairs," and "where youth grows pale, and spectre-thin and dies."

The line about dying youth refers to all men and women who pass away young, but it has a particular referent as well. Keats is clearly thinking about his brother Tom whom he nursed after he became ill with tuberculosis. Keats wants to be the sort of poet who can write persuasively about delight: "A thing of beauty is a joy forever," he famously begins his early poem *Endymion*. But he also wants to grow to the point where he can write about the sorrow to which all flesh is heir. He admires Wordsworth's capacity to do so: "His genius is explorative of those dark passages," says Keats in the maiden thought letter. In time, Keats will write brilliantly if obliquely about the passage of time and the pains of loss. No one who has once read the closing lines of "Ode to Autumn" is likely to forget them.

But Keats wants more than the capacity to write about the sorrows of the world. He clearly wants to be able to experience them and respond with humane compassion. He wants to come to some understanding about what suffering is and how it is best dealt with. Like Tom (and like his mother before Tom) Keats also contracted tuberculosis. During his illness he had to envision the loss of his beloved Fanny Brawne and imagine all the poems he would never have the chance to write. This he does with a dignity that is modest and self-aware and irrevocably moving. "Here lies one," his self-composed epitaph will say, "whose name was writ in water." He became the man that his poetry and his letters imagined into being. Poetry was his vocation, but it was also his school. I will call the world a "vale of soul-making," Keats says in another letter. And through his writing he made it precisely that.

When I was in college I took a drawing class. Why, I'm not really sure. Maybe it was that Bennington, the school I was attending, was an artistic sort of school and I felt the need to do something in art. I was simply terrible. My still life of dishes and pots and drapes did not look like the dishes and pots and drapes nor did it look unlike them in an interesting way. My nudes were all skinny shaky lines. When the models came off their pedestals and saw what I had done to them, they shook their heads in sorrow. But I tried. I smudged charcoal, wore down pencils, and ruined paper. I had the kind of fertility one associates with Picasso—five, ten drawings in an hour. (Drawing is easy if you don't know how.) I had the fertility one associates with Picasso, but a few of the other qualities seemed to be missing.

At the end of the term I had a conference with my teacher. She had won my heart on the first day of class by telling a story about how she began her life as an artist (a story which I shall elaborate rather freely). She had grown up in rural Vermont, and one day when she was a very young girl—three years old, four?—her parents told her that an important guest was coming. His name was Robert Frost. My teacher felt that this Robert Frost might be related in some way to a more important and more enduring being by the name of Jack Frost. Jack was to her the spirit of winter. He scattered the snowflakes from his palms and painted the windows white and sent the wind running loose over the sheeted fields and all the rest. She drew him and drew him and drew him, as she imagined him to be. The arrival of the actual man, perhaps the best American poet of his time (ask him—he would tell you, albeit archly enough), was a letdown, and his interest in the drawings wasn't what my teacher-to-be had hoped. But once begun on the artist's path there wasn't any stopping her.

So this kindly and rather high-spirited person, who was not much older than I, sat down and looked with me through my jungle of lines and shades and listened as I told her that I couldn't, wasn't, and never would. What she said went something like this: "You have no facility as a visual artist. You have none whatsoever. And this disturbs you." I agreed that it did.

"It's a mistake," she said. "It shouldn't." She told me that if I devoted myself to the medium of drawing I'd soon learn to create more plausible sketches. I would in time be able to draw a cat that looked like a cat—though maybe not one that anyone would expect to up and meow. I would learn to render shapes much as I'd learned (much as we'd both learned) to put sentences together and to write (and to think) more or less grammatically. But something else entirely would determine how far I would go as an artist.

It's the spirit that's in you that matters most, she said. It may take longer to express itself if the medium you choose is one you aren't naturally fluent in. You might come into your own faster using words than you would using forms and shapes—but you'll go about the same distance either way. It depends on your commitment to growth. I was twenty-one; I'd never heard the like of this. She said a lot of artists had to fight against their facility. She observed that a writer's glibness could stop him from cutting deep and getting to the serious matters he might want to express, as can a writer's sense of humor.

(Nietzsche, who didn't come into the conversation that day, was always suspicious of facility and though at times quite funny was nervous about joking. A joke, he said, is the epitaph for the death of a feeling.) An artist's fluency with his pencil could turn him into a mere illustrator, someone who created generic images allied with commonplace perception. A facile writer would always have a chance to sell the works of his pen—and that could corrupt him quickly. The gifted illustrator would face the same perils. These perils, my teacher and I agreed, would not be mine. They would not be mine in the visual arts and, as it turned out, they would not be mine in verbal endeavors either.

But my teacher's idea—which Keats would not, I think, reject out of hand—has stayed with me. I liked then and still like the notion that a medium—paint or clay or words—can be a medium for something called spirit or soul. I like the idea that mastering the medium is important, but that it's not the ultimate task. Keats's early poetry wasn't abominable quite. But it flirted with extreme badness. No one who reads the first volume he published (and that gleaned those horrible reviews) could ever imagine what kind of work he would produce and how quickly. Did Keats simply learn his craft at a stunning velocity? He did I think. But it was the need to express something—something in and of his spirit—that compelled him to move so quickly and to achieve so much. The spirit needed a way to make itself known in the world—or so at least I, a lover and maybe an idealizer of Keats and his poetry, am inclined to believe.

The growth from *Endymion* to "Ode to Autumn" is an artistic growth, but it is a growth of spirit, too. Melville said that a whaling ship was his Harvard and his Yale. Keats used poetry as his school, and it addressed his mind and his heart. He left with the highest conceivable honors.

He expanded. Early in his career, Keats could only write persuasively about a few matters: spring, beauty, pleasure. But as time went on and he exerted himself further, his powers expanded. He became someone who knew what to say when faced by loss and by death—and by love. Most of us cannot do that. When we fall in love or lose someone we adore, we are struck mute. But growth as a writer can in time allow one to face the most complex and powerful experiences and turn them into words. Keats passed from being able to write about happiness to being able to write about almost anything in words that are fresh and full of feeling. He used words to become himself. He used words to grow. Faced with death, a human being wants to be able to say more than "she's gone." Faced with love, he wants to say more than "she's beautiful." A real writer can say more, and the more makes his life something singular and true and more worth living than it would be if he remained mute, or spoke only in generalities and echoes.

But Keats is Keats. Can the rest of us send ourselves to the school of writing and emerge new men or new women? Surely it is not easy and few of us may be able to complete the whole course; that is few of us will let writing lead us as far as it can or will into unfolding what is best in ourselves. But I persist in thinking that no one who devotes a life to writing and uses it as Keats did to make better the self that genes and fate have given him will be entirely frustrated by what he can achieve. Whether the world itself is always a "vale of soul-making" is uncertain. But writing, entered into in the right spirit, is and always will be, at least for a spirit like John Keats.

TO FAIL

MELVILLE SAID IT memorably. He told the world that insofar as he was free of his obligations to his purse—his need to make money and keep mammon half content—he was dedicated to writing those works the world inevitably called failures. He evokes of *Moby-Dick* of course, which was neglected by many reviewers and generally misunderstood by the few who deigned to take note. Melville began his writing life as a smash success with a couple of novels about his travels in the exotic Pacific islands, *Typee* and *Omoo*. The writer who brought those books out was young and dashing and fresh from his own Pacific sojourn. The literary world made much of him. He didn't have a run quite like Lord Byron's, our exemplar of the erotic writer—this was Puritan America after all—but for a while Melville got close to being an American celebrity.

But something in him rebelled against it. He began to write more poetry—and Melville's poetry is wonderful, but not for everyone. His fiction became radically demanding. His audience felt like he had sold them out. The young entertainer was becoming something else. It was an insult, an affront to those who had loved his early work. They turned their backs on him and that seemed to push him further.

Melville might have gathered himself and reconsecrated his work. He might have let his audience—rather than his strong imagination—shape what he was going to do. But Melville didn't. He repaired with his family to a farmhouse in Pittsfield, Massachusetts, the far western part of the state, and went to work full bore on *Moby-Dick*. He wrote the book in a blue heat, flying along, hour after hour, sometimes as though it were being dictated to him from some other world. He wrote it fast. It took about fourteen months by one account and when he finished he felt he had been purified. I've written a wicked book, he told his friend Hawthorne, and now I feel spotless as the lamb.

The public didn't care for Melville's demonic book. The American reading classes were not up to it. They didn't have room for an orating sea captain whose nearly insane hunger for conquest and revenge and the great white whale predicted so many part-mad American quests to come. In Ahab's eyes you could catch the gleam that would put America in war after war, compel it to annihilate its Indian population, expand west and south, and then, in time, hunger to take the entire world under its eagle's spread wings. Melville predicted Vietnam and he predicted Iraq and he predicted the slaughter of the rebel armies in the Philippines and the murder of the Indians at Wounded Knee and everyplace else the tribes went down in senseless slaughter. And he predicted our hypocrisies, too. Ahab sometimes believes that his quest is *noble*. He sometimes seems to think himself a knight errant going off to rid the world of the predator beast, leviathan. His contradictions became our own. We are the nation who sought to create an empire for liberty.

What an amazing thought! An empire that would bring freedom to those we conquered and exploited. What a beautiful dream, having it both ways was. Melville's murderous multiracial crew is the harbinger of the multiracial American army that traverses the globe, blowing human beings to fleshy bits in order to save them.

Melville saw into the future in ways that his contemporaries never could have. (And in a way it's not hard to forgive them for their incapacity.) It took history (and us) some time to catch up with Melville's vision—Melville's failure.

As to Melville himself, he did not always take his lack of success in stride. He'd had his run with the great bitch goddess Success, as Henry Adams liked to call her, and it is not hard to understand why he wanted at least one taste more. With the vast novel about the whale, he surely must have felt he earned it. But Melville had to live with what over time seemed to him a rank failure. He went broke. For a long while he stopped writing. Some of the work he did manage stayed in the dark. "Bartleby, the Scrivener" was another piece of dire prophecy. The man who sits at his desk stubbornly preferring not to is a parody and a patron saint to every oppressed office worker from then to now who sits and dreams and broods and detests his life. The office slavery that Melville captured in that tale has become the order of much of the civilized world. Melville knew it. Melville knew it before we did or even could have. Prophet? Yes, but what the teacher said is true. Prophets are not honored in their own land or in their own time either. The future bears them out—or it does not.

Truly original writers, it's been said, must create the taste by which they will be appreciated. This Melville did. It was just that the taste-creation process took about a hundred years. And

Melville suffered for it during his life. He didn't only want readers in the future; he wanted readers in the present, now. Some people said his failure, or what he perceived to be failure, drove him nearly mad. He surely became deeply melancholy. He surely came close to giving up writing altogether. But he did have enough faith to finish *Moby-Dick* and in time to do more work. "Bartleby" is a wonder—and then came *Billy Budd*.

And I suspect that despite the sorrows there were other times in which Herman Melville's main sentiment was defiance. He was surely feeling defiant enough that day he spoke to the far more timid Hawthorne about the demonic whaling book. Melville was Ahab's creator after all, and I think he partook in Ahab's faith that the best way to confront a bitter, predatory world is to strike back at it—or to hit first. "Thy right worship," Ahab says, "is defiance." *Moby-Dick* was a defiant book, far darker than anything America was ready for, and Melville not only paid the price for his defiance but also reaped the bracing pleasures. After Melville died, the story goes, they came to move his desk. Carved far back on the great wooden vessel, the vessel that had gone over all those seas with the writer, were written some words from a poem by Friedrich Schiller. They were simple and direct: "Hold fast to the dreams of your youth."

But I'm not Herman Melville, you might say. I don't want to dare failure the way he did. I can't revel in possible failure in Melville's way. "No! I am not Prince Hamlet nor was meant to be," T. S. Eliot's Prufrock says, "am an attendant lord, one that will do to swell a progress." How many of us feel worthy of a Melville-like destiny? He was great and we are small. There is no reason to court failure the way Melville did. The probability is that we will fail twice. We'll fail once in the present (as Melville did) and then again in perpetuity. No bad books are remembered down through time, Auden said; but many good ones are forgotten. Chances are that one way or another we will be forgotten. No, we are not Prince Hamlet, nor Herman Melville either.

But Herman Melville was not Herman Melville, at least to begin with. He became so over time and well after he died. When he lived he was simply another writer trying to achieve what he could. He was overshadowed by numberless less accomplished figures; he was shunned by his publishers; he was insulted and maligned and all the rest. He was also loved and supported. Even in his darkest days he had friends, or at least some of them. But he did not know for certain that it was his destiny to live on through time. When he said he was devoted to failures, he meant that he was out to write books that were so large in scope, so ambitious and so original that they would have to fail, at least in some measure. No human being could realize the project that was *Moby-Dick* to perfection. There was joy in this feeling of taking on matters that were too big. Attacking something massive raised up a warrior's spirit in Melville. Emerson talks about the how young men sitting in libraries read the works of the great who have come before them and cower at their originality and force. What they forget is that those great authors were once young men sitting in libraries themselves. But they did not do much cowering—or if they did, they overcame it in time.

Part of the dignity of writing is that it allows men and women to take on tasks that may seem overwhelming and then do their best knowing that what's being attempted can't but end with some measure of failure. The critic Randall Jarrell once defined a novel as an extended fictional narrative with which something significant is wrong. In general it is more than merely one thing. You can keep yourself awake all night counting up Charles Dickens's literary crimes and misdemeanors: the sentimentality, the sloppiness, the overwriting, the sententiousness. But then you get up from your half slumber and read the opening passage of *Great Expectations* or *Bleak House* and you know that what he achieves is still magic. You are in his world in an instant and you do not want to leave.

One is tempted to echo Eliot. Good writers borrow; great writers steal. We might say that good writers fail small time; great writers are constantly failing at a rather grand level. If you're not failing, you're probably not setting your sights high enough. I know there are some works that we think of as flawless: Jane Austen's and Alexander Pope's come to mind. And they are wonderful writers, but put beside them Charles Dickens and that massive failure John Milton (God's lines in the great poem are beyond being merely embarrassing) and they become something a bit less. It's wonderful to see chunky Babe Ruth whack one out of the park. But he misses the ball with almost the same relish as he slams it. The swing is all.

Writing is always a lost cause. To stay with baseball for a second, you can always see much further than you can hit. You've read the very best of literary artists and you know you are not there, cannot get there today, maybe will never get there. But this knowing lends dignity to what you're up to. You've entered a world in which there are no limits to excellence—and accordingly a world where everyone fails and there is failure everywhere.

Mailer is not Melville, but on the subject of failure the sage of Brooklyn has some worthwhile thoughts. Mailer was a devoted reader of his reviews and in time he became a close student of what reviews meant about the nature of a book. He suggested that if your reviews broke 60 percent thumbs up and 40 down, then that was fine. He implied that probably the reverse was OK, too. Though he knew that when matters went that way his next advance would suffer. But Mailer also suggests that when the reviews are unremittingly positive, you haven't done what you should have. You haven't pushed hard enough against the boundaries of conventional opinion and conventional consciousness. In other words, if you have succeeded too well you haven't failed nearly well enough.

I've only had one book that was anything like an across-the-board critical success. It was called *Teacher* and its ostensible subject was a terrific and very eccentric philosophy teacher that I and my buddies were lucky enough to have at our proletariat high school. (Its non-ostensible subject? Growing up. America. The sixties. Rock music. My father.) Man, did reviewers love that book. I must have grabbed around forty reviews, almost all positive—with some gushers thrown in. Never have I been so much kissed in print. Everyone seemed to like that book, which made me feel grand—and also crummy. I'd read Melville; I'd listened a little to the sage of Brooklyn. I wanted to write books, not Hallmark cards.

In time I was rescued. It turned out there was a constituency who hated *Teacher*—or at least looked at it with a wary eye. Teachers! Many teachers who picked up the book were made unhappy by it. In the war of us against them, kids versus teachers, I was too much of the party of the kids it turned out. I'd aligned myself with the kids in their rank rebellion against the way it was and the way it had to be. I was using my adult mind and my expensive education to say in rather more polished ways what the students at every slave-system high school coughed into their sleeves. Down with boredom. Down with submasters and disciplinarians and the people who're running a jail when they pretend to be running a school. The great thing about our teacher Frank Lears was that he was not really a teacher at all. He was one of us. Real teachers read the book—it was a frequent Christmas present to them I fear—and they let loose some bile.

I heard about it—letters and e-mails and stand-up well-rehearsed harangues at lectures. I took it with a smile. You might even say that I was happy. I knew I wasn't playing for the biggest stakes. But finally the oddly delectable, acrid burnt-coffee scent of failure had entered the room.

TO CHANGE THE WORLD

SHOULD YOU TRY to change the world—or some small corner of it—with your writing? Ultimately every young writer must decide if she will make the attempt. Writers achieve gains for themselves, or they try. As we've said, they can develop their minds and expand their spirits, and they can fail in the most satisfying and profitable ways. But what about the writer and the world outside her head and heart? Can writers change the world? Should they even try?

Percy Bysshe Shelley was accused once of writing books for the purpose of changing the world. Shelley wasn't long in responding. He wanted to know exactly what purpose his detractor had when he wrote his books (or his essays, or his squibs). Ultimately, Shelley asked what purpose there could be to writing if not to change the world.

Shelley was that way. Every time he picked up his pen, he was out to save humanity. He believed in the transforming power of literature; he told us at the end of his treatise in defense of poetry that "poets are the unacknowledged legislators of the world." Well, after Shelley they shouldn't be unacknowledged anymore. According to Shelley, everyone should understand that much of what we call human progress owed and owes to the exertions of imaginative writers.

How do writers change the world? For one thing, they reinvigorate the language. If poets don't come along with their metaphors and their verbal twists and turns, then language will become inert. It will be dead, as Shelley says, "to all the nobler purposes of human intercourse." Language is the most intimate medium of human exchange and it must be kept vital. Language must reflect the mystery, beauty, and sadness of life. Those are abiding facts, and when language flattens out, we can no longer perceive them.

Literature is also a source of virtue, or so Shelley says. In the great books we come up close to images of the best of all possible human beings; we meet the ideals of a good or true or beautiful life. Shelley tried to offer such images himself all through his career. His paragon of humane excellence is Prometheus, the hater of tyrants: not only a poet but also a scientist, architect, physician, and inventor whose contributions transform human life for the better. For Shelley all forms of productive invention are related to poetry. The source of great writing is imagination to be sure. But scientists and rulers who genuinely want to help mankind draw on the same ennobling faculty. They conceive the world not only as it is, but (through imagination) as it ought to be, and they work for the necessary changes.

Above all Shelley was an apostle of freedom. Everywhere he looked he saw that his fellow men and women were in chains—and he did what he could to help snap them. But the chains were not always material. Often they were what Blake, who would have loved Shelley's work had he read it, would have called "mind-forg'd manacles." For Shelley believed he had made a discovery. People were addicted to their own servitude: over time they came to love being in thrall to this absolute power or that. They were often physically constricted but the constrictions that mattered most were mental. And Shelley believed that by writing with passion, energy, and daring, he could liberate his readers. He wrote to spread the truth and to change the world.

His Prometheus isn't only oppressed by the gods; he's also oppressed by himself. Chained on the rock, Shelley's Prometheus is the victim of the horrid god Jupiter's wrath, but he's also the victim of his own. When we first encounter Prometheus (who is surely a version of Shelley) he is suffering harshly and a bit operatically. "Ah me," he says, "pain ever, forever." Not only is he locked down to a rock in the barren Caucasus Mountains but also every day an eagle comes to feed on his liver. What keeps Prometheus going at the outset of the poem is knowing that his foe's days are numbered. A prophecy has told them both that one day Jupiter will fall. Prometheus spends his time pining for that day, and imagining what horrors he'll inflict on Jupiter once he, Prometheus, rules the world.

Shelley's implications in this, perhaps the greatest of romantic poems, are clear. As soon as he ascends, Prometheus will set to work becoming a Jupiter figure. He'll torture Jupiter in the same way and eventually with the same thrill with which Jupiter tortured him. Prometheus is in thrall. He's in thrall to the horrible king of the universe, but he's also in thrall to his spirit of revenge. He doesn't want freedom; he's not pining for the liberty to create and to love. Those matters are at best secondary. He's pining for the chance to exact revenge and to get the whole cycle of domination, submission, and rebellion going again. In the course of the magnificent poem, Prometheus will learn better. He'll see that the true reward for breaking free from Jupiter's chains is anything but becoming another Jupiter. He'll make himself into a genuinely loving and creative figure and what he achieves society may achieve along with him.

Everywhere men and women are in chains. It's a sentiment that's close to Shelley's heart—and almost all the romantic writers share it. In their different ways Wordsworth and Coleridge and Keats and Whitman and Emerson and Thoreau and Emily Dickinson all wrote to break chains. Dickinson wrote in part to liberate herself from the oppressions of her Puritan faith and straitlaced culture: but many readers who have encountered her over time have been set free from their own bonds—or so they felt. The romantics write to enfranchise men and women. Romantics write to change the world.

But the poets are not the only professed chain breakers. Rousseau and Marx, two of the major political thinkers of the modern period, also saw humanity in chains; the metaphor occurs and reoccurs in their work. For Marx the manacles are forged by capitalism; in Rousseau the culprit is society with its rules and regulations and its swerve away from the humane and just life that nature offers. Rousseau and Marx both wanted to change the world. They wrote to liberate; they wrote to enfranchise.

There are not many now who will say that Marx did the world palpable good; most will, in fact, say quite the opposite. And Rousseau? He is still esteemed in France. Almost all French writers who have achieved any measure of renown are still esteemed in France. But few of our contemporaries can rest easy with his view that human beings are *naturally* good—not after Darwin, not after Auschwitz. And his centrality to the men who fomented the French Revolution and sent streams to the guillotine will always make him suspect.

Face it. We now often look askance at writers who think of themselves as chain breakers. We are not comfortable with scribbling liberators of mankind. So many of the monsters of the last two centuries have come to us trailing their ideologies, their cruelties, and the books they authored to make it all seem justified. Somewhere in an ugly squat of hell Mao waves the Little Red Book; Hitler reads aloud from *Mein Kampf*; Lenin rages on about imperialism and the death throes of capitalism. Perhaps Rousseau and Marx are there with them.

Are Blake and Shelley on hand too: not for the content of their doctrine, which is humane and generous, but rather for their hubris? For by writing to change the world they contributed to the pernicious illusions that books and authors really are the legitimate legislators—rather than, say, custom and usage. Or maybe they are there in hell simply because they asked too much of humanity—when we all know that one of the best ways to make people explode in resentment and then maybe succumb to regression is to make demands they cannot fulfill. Sublimation—the turning of basic energies into refined, civilizing energies—can only go so far the psychiatrists tell us. Eventually the old demons break through and often with redoubled force.

"Poetry makes nothing happen," W. H. Auden famously said. By which I think he means that true poetry, the sort he aspired to write, makes nothing happen. Authentic writing makes nothing happen in part because it can never be confused with propaganda. Poetry—real poetry—is too enmeshed in complexities ever to be turned into policy. Auden can be a didactic poet, no doubt. (Saying that poetry makes nothing happen and saying so in the midst of an elegy for Yeats is evidence.) But Auden was a close enough student of politics and history to see that it was raw simplicities that most often swayed the world. He once declared that a person who felt he had a lot to say—a good deal of advice to dispense to humanity—would probably amount to nothing much as a poet. Rather, Auden said, it was the sort of person who liked to play with words to see what they might be able to do and how they could sound together that would have the best chance to write poetry, or at least to write poems that W. H. Auden would want to read.

Well, you may say, that was Auden. But—if one can venture a generalization this large—most postromantic writers of consequence have followed his lead, the lead of writers we call modernist. Virginia Woolf wrote a partially admiring essay about Shelley in which she said that he was "not one of us." By "us" she probably meant most all women and men, who cannot readily say of themselves what Shelley once did of himself: "I go until I am stopped and I never am stopped." But Woolf was also talking about the denizens of Bloomsbury, her fellow artists and writers, who were prone to be ironic, urbane, and interested more in cultivating their own gardens and developing the rigors of their art than in changing the world. The headlong nature of Shelley's art was anything but Bloomsburyan.

Do writers now want to change the world? Should they? I think most writers now shy away from the great romantic project, which comes along with multiple risks. They are afraid of sounding too grand; they are afraid of being mocked. They write from their own vantage point—but they resist the general perspective. They don't talk about "we"—both as we are now and as we might with work and luck become—in the way

Shelley and Whitman so freely did. Even those writers who want to do more than entertain are cautious, tapping ahead like unsighted men and women over uneven ground.

They're nervous. How can they speak for all when, as they see it, we're all so different? Maybe there is one truth for women and one for men. Maybe the black truth is not the white. And maybe the Asian truth subverts both. What about the times in which we live and how they condition our perceptions, maybe to the point of determining them? What's so now will be untrue tomorrow—and in need of being unsaid. Wittgenstein made a famous claim: The world is all that is the case. But won't what is the case and what makes up the world shift and slide like a city built on water and sand? Writing that describes a far-gone and past world—and the news media tell us the world is new every fifteen minutes, or after the next commercial interruption—can't be of any value and can only in time be a humiliation to the author.

Does anyone write to change the world anymore? Does anyone still write to break the chains?

I think they should. William Carlos Williams said that he understood it was hard to get the "news" out of poems—especially, he implied, modern poems like his and those of his lifelong friend and antagonist, Ezra Pound. The poems tend to be difficult and dense and (in Pound's case) frighteningly allusive. But, Williams went on to say, it's important to keep at it; for men and women die miserably every day for lack of what is found in poetry. He wasn't talking about poems that feature the poet, the teakettle, and the kitchen curtains. He was talking about poems of sweep and daring, poems that come in like thunderstorms at sea and send the waves into a reeling dance and make the clouds leap in the sky. Williams wrote some of those poems, or at least he tried. He tried in his own behalf and, as his famous line shows, he tried in behalf of his readers.

Prophetic writers have done their harm. The ones who have seen themselves as coming down from Sinai with a tablet in hand rather than down from the attic with a fat yellowed manuscript have sometimes made mischief. But it is not as though without writers there would be no mischief.

Without some waking up, human beings would die of self-suffocation; they'd lie down and push the pillow over their own heads and press, press, press. The spirit of the self takes us over very easily. We are inclined to back away into existences that are not much better than animal. We horde and sleep and feed. We become creatures of appetite, not much more. Writers say everything under the sun. But I think that all real writers are constantly saying one thing. Wake up!

Wake up: stop sleepwalking. Put an end to the death in life, the comatose come-along that most of us engage in most of the time. Wake up and smell the coffee, the flowers, and the air. (To breathe the air is sheer delight, says Shelley—or at least it can be after Prometheus effects his revolution.) Wake up! And then what? Well, what you do when you open your eyes is up to you. But, the writer (the real writer) continues, I do have a few ideas.

HITTING YOUR STRIDE:
PERILS AND PLEASURES /
PLEASURES AND PERILS

PERILS AND PLEASURES

TO DRINK

WRITERS DRINK. THERE'S no way around that. They do. It's one of the main perils of writing. Writers as a class probably drink less than they once did, but they can still hold their own against most any professional group, no matter how bibulous. They do drugs too and for all sorts of reasons. But why do they? And should you?

Alcohol is a mystery drug. We don't really know what it does for the imbiber, either on the psychological level or the physiological. If there is a more puzzling everyday mystery than what happens when people get high (a little or a lot) on alcohol, I'm not sure what it is. I do think, though, that we can say something general about what happens when you take in smallish amounts of booze: one drink, two, or (if you happen to possess a stevedore build) maybe three. But probably not three. No, probably not. The poet George Herbert tells us to avoid the third glass and there's almost certainly something in what he says.

It's hard to avoid the third glass, though, especially when you use alcohol the way I think many writers do. They use it to relax. All day they've been using and overusing a muscle, their minds. And rather than getting looser, as bodily muscles will, the muscle that is (metaphorically) the mind seems to have a tendency to grow tighter with focused (and often profitable) use. The basketball jock and the tennis player exhaust the muscles of their bodies and when they're done, so long as they haven't pushed themselves too far, feel pretty good. They get what people like to call "deliciously tired." They sprawl out on the old gray overstuffed and they listen to some music or watch TV or read a book or simply claim a benignly vegetative state. This according to many is happiness.

Mental exertion seems a bit different. If you've figured out your entry protocols—your meditation, your drink of choice, your nonfattening chocolate bar (which someone should invent soon)—then your initial feeling on sliding into your work is loose and easy. You're on the field; you're warmed up and ready to play. And play it can be. When the ideas are rolling out and somehow the (approximately) right words are appearing and forming (roughly) the right order, then you feel a little like you're flying. And even if you're not flying or even gliding yet, there's still a sense of untapped energy. The wind is in your sails, and all that.

This goes on. The wind lasts for different lengths of time for different people. For a given individual it may vary day to day. While the breeze blows it's all lovely. But then, imperceptibly, the breeze cuts back a little and you have to start rowing. Rowing strains the back and the legs and the gut, but the craft is still sliding forward and all's well. But then it gets hard. It gets very hard. You taste the sweat on your face and the oar blisters your hand. You're puffing. And so it can be with writing. You're sailing, but then in time you have to push it. You have to row.

Even if you have the sense to quit before you melt down completely, you've still tired out your mind and probably your spirit, too. And there you encounter one of the catches of writing: it doesn't always relax the mind the way physical exertion relaxes the body. The elastics get tighter and tighter rather than loosening. Why this is I'm not sure.

No doubt there are writers who finish a pair of sessions in a day and feel cleansed and pure and ready to go off and do complex math in their heads. But I'm guessing not. What comes after the writer's play and work is often painful mental compression. Writing can intensify the tensions in the mind to a potent degree.

Writer's tension doesn't only come from exertion it seems to me. There's also the pressure of doubt. Is this any good? Should I keep working on it? Am I wasting my time? For the novelist, this must be an especially tough issue. For novelists, practiced as they might be, are always liable to make wrong turns. Suddenly the love interest's car veers off the road and into the ditch—ambulance, emergency room, doctor, body cast. Body cast! Body cast? Was that really such a good idea? A body cast has the power of inhibiting a plot as well as anything. But I've gone twenty pages down the body-cast path. To backtrack or not to backtrack? There's cause for a headache.

Now add some financial insecurity to your mind fatigue and artistic worry. You're hearing the ping of e-bills as you write. Add a daughter with a high-mucus cold and a son whose proclivity to share toys at day care by flinging them at other kids has been revealed only yesterday afternoon. Enough said.

And, as all writers know, there is an elixir that can relax those tensions with a few swallows, then a few more. It really is something like magic. Writing long and hard the mind becomes aching and taut. But then, a little like Alice on her journey through Wonderland, we come upon a magic bottle that says DRINK ME. (Actually we know very well where the bottle is.) We do, and the iron hand that's been squeezing our brain relaxes its hold a little. I'm not always sure why the Greeks made devious Hermes a god; and jealous Hera can be exasperating, always running down Zeus to spoil his fun. But two or three swallows of red wine after a hard day's writing and I am ready to contribute to the building of a local temple for Lord Dionysus.

Damn is red wine good stuff. (Recast that sentence using your own drink of choice and see how well it works.) I even like the red wine that comes in flagon-sized bottles and that's what I drink most of the time. Twelve bucks' worth—lasts me three nights—no it lasts four, five, honest. But I don't need prime vintage. I'm with that character in Iris Murdoch who had only one thing—one thing only—against a dear friend. She introduced him to high-priced, grand-tasting red wine, which made his day-to-day vintage (the vintage he could afford) seem dull. It's red wine itself that's wonderful and Lord Bacchus be praised for even its modest manifestations. As to the top-shelf stuff, I'll drink it from time to time. Good wine is my default celebration flourish. But really, I'm always most happy to return to backbench, down-home, plain and simple red. Lord Bacchus, be praised one more time!

The drug is magic. It does what the imaginary label says it is supposed to do. It makes calm what was turbulent; it makes soft what was steel; it slacks the ropes and lets drift the craft. If any drug was ever concocted for the weary writer it must be wine. It's as though Bacchus, a junior god, made a kind offering to his older brother, Apollo, lord of arts and artists. This is for all,

Bacchus might have said, but especially for your children, children of the reed. (Or pen.) What Apollo gave in return I'm not sure, but it could not have been small.

Wine (or beer or whatever) loosens the screws, and they can get awfully tight. That's one glass. That's two. But then the *peril*.

One glass, two—it gives you more than relaxation. It gives you something just as important. Wine (or whatever) gives you a dose of self-acceptance.

Let's say—along with Freud and Plato and plenty of other thinkers—that human beings are not unified in their inner lives. Let's say we're made of relatively separate pieces, relatively separate agencies. Freud called them the I, the over-I, and the it. Plato called them mind, spirit, and appetite. At the very least, almost everyone who has seriously considered the question understands human beings to be creatures split at least in two. The dualists see us as divided between nature and culture or between nature and God. Plato and Freud are more complicated (and for my money, more illuminating). To most who have paused to think hard about it, we are not united creatures. We want more than one thing at a time and those wants collide to create confusion (Plato) and anxiety (Freud). Division hurts. In Freud the I wants to survive, the over-I wants perfection, and the it wants all the pleasure it can get. One can readily see the problems that inevitably arise. We're three-headed beings clamoring (and sometimes whispering and sometimes scheming) for three (at least three) different objectives.

It's not surprising that we seek unity. For in unity we find calm. Plato says the exercise of reason can bring us such calm, but admits there are few who exercise reason terribly well. Freud says calm is the exception, not the rule and we have to learn to live with internal discomfort. Being human means accepting a measure of anxiety. Writers tend to be lively, even turbulent spirits—hungry for life, hungry for the perfection of their work, and aware (sometimes) of their need to get on in the world. The agitators in the machine can seem to churn without ceasing.

A passionate nature, the fatigue of writing, and the desire for some resolution and calm: no wonder writers and artists of all types (as well as people who think the first step in becoming an artist is to get messed up a lot) are prone to drink. And—marvel of marvels—it works. One glass of wine, then another (or the equivalent), sipped slowly creates a soft sea of tranquility. As my former teacher David Lenson describes the experience of being a little buzzed in his great book *On Drugs*: "What *is* simply *is*." But when we have the couple of cups, we are (to get a little high flow about it) like a Moses who has seen the promised land and maybe stepped foot inside. We want to stay there. We want to abide forever in the sphere of self-acceptance and calm. And then our troubles begin. Gore Vidal expresses the hunger for inebriation trenchantly, if darkly enough. In Michael Mewshaw's *Sympathy for the Devil*, Vidal speaks of the desire "to sink myself into whiskey where one's sense of time is so altered that one feels in the moment immortality—a long luminous present which, not drinking, becomes a fast-moving express train named . . . Nothing." Did Vidal bemoan the fact that he was always a godfather never a god? It seems that drink made him feel just a bit more deific.

There have been many fine observations about getting high—that is, elevating ourselves over the human landscape of bumps and ruts, sorrow and pain, and then cruising along as if on wings. But there is none in my view to touch a line by

George Carlin, which I'll adapt to the subject at hand. Glass of wine, great stuff. Makes a new man out of you. Only one problem: new man wants a glass. (New woman does too.) Once we've touched the promised land of peace and plenty, we want to stay there, or go deeper inside and so the perils begin. The only paradises are lost paradises the man says. And a booze buzz makes us feel that we are returning to some life of fullness and plenty (in the womb, in Mom's arms?) that we've lost. New woman wants a drink. New man does, too.

And if your inner life is especially active, if the weather front tends to shift four or five times a day, then no doubt a little release feels fine. And then it fades and you go running after what you had like a kid who's lost his grip on the tail of a gorgeous kite of many colors. Trouble begins.

And the trouble can continue on a long way. Booze gives us a dose of happy consciousness, and that's not so easy to find. But booze can also deliver smashed dishes, smashed cars, smashed marriages. Booze has been compared to rope, for which there are many fine uses. You can use it to secure ship to shore; you can use it to tie the load on tight; you can have a high-spirited tug of war with it, too. But you can also put a hangman's noose in your rope and throw it over a branch or a beam. And then what happens does. As Lenson says in *On Drugs*, "Beneath alcohol's icons and institutions lie its familiar wastes: broken glass, a body in the gutter, the wreckage of cars, promises, families, and dreams."

Booze creates all sorts of troubles, from great to small, starting of course with the hangover. One glass extra, two or three too many and you begin waking up with mild and not so mild symptoms of flu. You've got a dose of what they used to call the ague. Tired, sore, dry throat, sluggish, irritable—

there you are. Does your husband have to jam so many of those loud consonants into his sentences? Does your wife need to sing with so much gusto? Ah, the hangover—a subject in itself, but for another time.

One might only say this. As grievous as a hangover can be, it has its advantages. It tends to make you hypersensitive, critical, suspicious, mildly annoyed at the world, and maybe a little more than mildly annoyed at yourself. It's the perfect state, in other words, to experience a certain difficult *pleasure*. It's the perfect state in which to revise your work.

Like many other facts of the midgame writer's life, drinking is a double-edged matter. At extremes it can quicken and it can kill; in moderation it can brighten a sallow world. But even in moderation booze is a complicated business, with all the twists and loops of a demon's tail.

Writing is full of glorious oases that turn out to be alive with toothy monsters, and those sites that appear to be nothing but woe can often yield unexpected possibilities. You're alone all the time—and that's often a trial. But when you get in the habit, and cultivate it well, loneliness can morph into deep pleasure at being alone. You have to change your ways of reading from complete and joyous immersion to something more detached, and that too can have its long-run satisfaction. As a spy in the world of the normal and the ostensibly nice, you'll sometimes be compelled to silence. But you'll be able to redeem that silence when you get back to your desk.

And the immediately good things about writing can have a dark underside. That book of yours that sells and sells can taint your mind in strange ways; that beautiful new word processor, your personal genie, can maim your possibilities as a writer but good.

The writer's middle distance is a land of ambiguities. There are no pleasures but a little pain comes along to salt them. Almost no losses but they have their salutary side.

The key, I think, is to develop a double vision that sees both dimensions of life and never to be terribly surprised when the sweet suddenly goes a note sour; and never to be shocked when what seems the worst turn reveals some expanding possibilities. To be a successful midgame writer, you have to master the art of what the poet of Hibbing, Minnesota, once claimed was the only thing he really knew how to do: keep on keeping on. (Like a bird that flew.)

TO GET REVIEWED

EMERSON DID NOT care for his reviews or his reviewers. He said once that when he looked up at the sky and took in the glories of the firmament and brooded on the majesty of the universe and of the bounties of the creator (I elaborate a touch here) then (and probably only then) could he forget that he had been reviewed. One knows the feeling. Reviews are a peril. Reviews—no matter how high hearted about it all one claims to be—are a danger. They're one of the reasons for writing it (whatever *it* may be) and putting it in the drawer, maybe not just for Horace's recommended nine years, but forever.

Reviews are an inevitable peril (by and large) in the writing game. But in times past one could hate or disdain or fear a select few sources: the human hatchets at *Newsweek*, the meat cleaver who chops bones for the *Post*, the hangmen at the *Times*. (A writer friend of mine comes to visit the newborn of mutual pals. The writer leans over the crib and intones a melancholy blessing: "May you never be reviewed by Michiko Kakutani.") But now everyone is a reviewer, thanks to the Internet and the democratizing of the review. And all can do it anonymously.

(Reviewing a book anonymously, Schopenhauer said, is not unlike addressing a political gathering wearing a mask.) The Internet gives license to galloping hordes of reviewers, where once there were but a few.

Said Heraclitus: Life is a child playing with dice: the game is to the child. Well, in the lifetime feud between writers and reviewers, the game is to the reviewers. From time to time someone on the writer's side will get a good one off. Martin Amis asked us to ponder the simple question: Is that what he wanted to be when he grew up? A reviewer? But that's a well-aimed sniper shot discharged from the concrete and steel wreckage; the reviewers deliver the bombs.

Even when they like—even when they love—what you've done, there is usually something at least slightly wrong with what they say. The review of your book describes something not unrelated to what you take yourself to have written. There are the characters; there are the themes; there is a word about the style that's not irrelevant to the book as you believe you know it. But something is wrong here. Something is badly wrong. They wrote about your book and they made it much smaller than it is. They made it much, much smaller. What they failed to see were the implications. They missed the ripple effect. They didn't understand how your book, though ostensibly about one thing, was actually about many things. In fact—whisper this; don't say it aloud—your book was about *everything*. Oh, it may ostensibly be just a memoir, but in that memoir was an implicit story of America, the whole shebang, circa the time of *you*. It was large. It contained multitudes—both spoken and implied.

That's what the bad reviewers do. That's what all but the very best reviewers do. They cut off the connotations.

The reviewers took Melville's gargantuan book (this is every writer's favorite example isn't it?) and they thought it was about whaling and in whaling it turned out they were not terribly interested. Nor did they expect the American literary public of 1851 to be. What they didn't see—the connotations, the resonance!—what they did not see was that this was a book about America. (Most all of our books are about America aren't they?) No reviewer will ever give you your penumbra, your halo, your ripple effect. Good books are about what they're about, but they're about more, too. Reviewers seem never to get to that "more." Melville's didn't; they left him angry and distressed. In time he wrote "Bartleby" about someone alone and unhappy and misunderstood, and he wrote *Billy Budd*, which would break the devil's heart if he chose to read it.

I've learned a great deal from my reviews says the magnanimous writer. Hah! Many writers stop reading their reviews at a certain point in their lives. They get their wives or husbands to give 'em the gist and that's enough. Sometimes they request the gist with a bit of sugar on top. It's said that Thomas Hardy's wife having read a review of her husband's latest in some shrine to literary respectability called out: "Thomas you have to read this. There are a great many fine criticisms of your work here." "Criticisms, criticism," Hardy purportedly said. "What I want is praise!" So Frost asked his readers and reviewers to be more responsive to the feats he accomplished in his poetry. "The whole thing is performance and prowess and feats of association," Frost said. "Why don't critics talk about those things— what a feat it was to turn that that way, and what a feat it was to remember that, to be reminded of that by this. Why don't they talk about that? Scoring. You've got to *score*. They say not, but you've got to score, in all the realms—theology, politics, astronomy, history, and the country life around you." Frost scored and scored, at least to his own mind (and mine). But the scoreboard the reviewers controlled never quite gave out the right totals.

Even a good review can leave you reeling and a great one (those exist, don't they?) can leave you growling quietly to yourself. (No one wants to hear those particular growls.) They shrink your book. And accordingly they shrink you. Whitman (as one cannot say too many times) had it right: he who touches this book touches a man. The book *is* the woman who wrote it, soul and body. We're all trying. We're all doing our best. Why don't reviewers understand as much and occasionally dispense the benefit of the doubt?

I quit writing reviews. I had sinned a few too many times (though not that many) against literary faith and love and the spirit of Melville. But during my reviewing time, who knows how many true writers I may have pushed off course, or gored so deeply that they had to spend a month on the couch waiting for the wound to close. I am sorry to one and all.

The writer James Atlas talks in his fine and undervalued memoir about what it was like to get his first (and only—mark that!) novel, *The Great Pretender*, reviewed. It was a set of killers: Lehmann-Haupt in the daily *Times*, Jonathan Yardley in the *Washington Post*, Leslie Fiedler in the *Times Book Review*, and the one that even thirty years down the line I still remember— Sven Birkerts's in the *New Republic*. There's a moment when Saul Bellow enters Atlas's book for a cameo. He places his hat down on the kitchen table. The hat! Bellow's hat! The narrator idolizes Bellow and the sight of the great man's haberdashery on the table propels him into a moment of bliss. Bellow's hat!

Birkerts's finding: The novel was timid as a cheese-seeking mouse in daytime, flat as your palm, and derivative, mostly derivative. It emerged from the Chicago laureate. It popped out of Bellow's hat.

The reviews were apparently about as easy for Atlas to get over as a case of dengue fever. Atlas started with a period where he was supine, suffering, and near delirious. Then he rose unsteadily and stumbled around the room and finally out into the light. But the thing about dengue—the thing about this bad review—was the recurrence factor. Atlas assumed that everyone he knew had read it. So when he emerged from sick bay, still shaky, he was always ready to hear a nasty crack from someone: always nervous, always distressed, and ever ready to cut and make a retreat. And some of his friends (so-called) did want to talk about the reviews. They wanted to congratulate him for being considered at length in the pages of prestigious journals. Or they wanted to discuss the nuances of the denunciation. They did not, in other words, want to do the one thing the author needed: forget it, or if not that, at least shut up about it.

Atlas took it all to heart. His invitations dwindled (and he knew why). Acquaintances crossed the street when he came trundling their way (and he knew what for). His phone sat silent as an abandoned black anvil, it being the days of black anvil phones I guess (and he knew the reason). No one asked for his next novel (and he knew why and this time maybe he was correct). And then he went on to write about it all in a funny, deft, absorbing memoir, in an often silver-throated voice, and probably got some redemption. Probably—*some* redemption.

Maybe the reason Atlas's life got bleaker was because he got bleaker: postreview he became more of a trench coated alone-goer, a Dostoyevskian lurker in his own life. And who wants to hang out with that guy? But still, one has to sympathize. He writes that "eventually after a few years of therapy, I came out of my depression." Years! Of therapy! Years!

I suppose you could say the nasty reviewers are the wolves that cull the herd. They lie in wait for the weak and unwary and pounce when the moment comes. They open up space for younger, or simply stronger (or more tone-deaf) aspirants to enter the writing game. They send the gimpy players off to the sidelines and exile them, sometimes permanently. Still, I cannot love reviewers. They can rarely imagine that the book they are reading is better than the books they have written or could write.

Yet see it from the reviewer's point of view. Buying a book and reading it is an investment: an investment of money, yes, but more than that an investment of time. Shouldn't readers be forewarned when they're on the verge of acquiring a lemon? If the fruit on the stand is rotten or the king is buck naked, shouldn't someone say so? A bad movie blots out two hours of your life; a bad novel can blacken two weeks. Yes, yes, I suppose so: there are reasons for bad reviews. But should the reviewers take such ostentatious joy in producing them? Denunciations are easy to compose (ask legions of secret police and spies). Praise is hard. One must be modest; one must admit the book (the woman, the man) is better than you are.

Don't laugh about the effects of rotten reviews. In his elegy for Keats, Shelley talks about the destructive power of the arrow that flies in darkness. He's referring to the negative and anonymous reviews that he suggests had a part in the early sickness and death of Keats. Northrop Frye, one of the wisest of critics, claims that Shelley is being figurative. What Shelley means to say is that the indifference and the disdain of the public can have an ill effect on writers. To which, lover of Frye that I am, I have to say: No, sorry, I don't think so. Shelley knows more than you do. That reviewer who told the young physician Keats to stop writing and get back to his pills and his camphor ought to have been brought up on charges. In a way, he was. Keats's older friend Hazlitt took him to task in an essay that will live eternally in the vindictive hall of fame. But that did nothing to save Keats.

Souls are like bodies; you can hurt them with a blow. Unearned violence against them can cause trauma. Earned violence can, too. I more than half believe that if it were not for those reviewers, Keats might have gotten sick later than he did. We might have had a few more poems like "To Autumn."

One believes in compassion. Freud said he was a godless Jew. As to me, I think of myself as a godless Christian. I believe in the teachings of Rabbi Jesus—or most of them—but not in worshipping the character who drowned the world because it annoyed him, and who wiped out the firstborn of all the Egyptians to show his might. So that means I believe in compassion. As Blake put it, "I forgive you, you forgive me / As our dear Redeemer said / 'This the Wine and this the Bread.'"

Still there are certain stories about encounters between reviewers and the reviewed that I don't mind hearing more than once. Dale Peck, a human hacksaw, reviewed Stanley Crouch's novel *Don't the Moon Look Lonesome*, and he did not care much for it. ("*Don't the Moon Look Lonesome* is a terrible novel, badly conceived, badly executed, and put forward in bad faith; reviewing it is like shooting fish in a barrel.") Crouch apparently caught sight of Peck at a restaurant in the Village, crossed the room, and identified himself. Crouch reached out his right hand and Peck took it. Crouch, who is a sturdy fellow, grasped hard and harder. With his left, he slapped Peck twice across the face, with force. Unfair, you'll say, uncouth. But isn't this a version of what reviewers sometimes do? Clasp your book in their hands, embrace it, and then slap you across the face?

I understand that the *Times* reviewer Michiko Kakutani (may you never be reviewed by MK) never disseminates her photo, rarely goes out in public, rarely makes herself known. No surprise—she has written some memorable appreciations. But all professional reviewers have it in them to be killers of souls, and she is no exception. Occasionally, just occasionally, they should have to answer.

Emerson was right and so was Shelley. The best reviews are tough to take: they're like dessert pies made of spinach and green beans. The worst are unspeakable. They're made of barbed wire and dead bolts. Eat them you must—even if because merely hearing of their existence, you up and compose them yourself. In general there are no great reviews and there are no great reviewers.

Oh, every now and then some large soul who does not frequently review makes his way into a periodical and writes with something like love in the heart. But once he has revealed the capacity, the authorities take care to have him eliminated in a midnight purge. From time to time a generous review gives true pleasure. The writer feels finally that one of his highest hopes has been fulfilled. He wrote to be *understood* and now at least one large soul has done it.

Too many reviews are studies in resentment. They condense the rancor of the reviewer who cannot write and calm the envy of those who wish to write and cannot. The reader of reviews will have to read between the lines to find out if he will actually enjoy the book and profit by it.

Writing is its own reward. Do not write with an eye forward to the day of publication and review. Write with an eye to the next word that you'll put down. Reviews are like divots in the playing field; insignificant in themselves they can still cause injuries if you let them.

Step out into nature, stare up at the teeming sky, full of stars that glow like the works of the writers who've come before us and inspire and incite; they are your true company, not the company of reviewers. (Melville shines down. Keats does and Shelley, too.) Follow Emerson. Forget you've been reviewed or ever will be. Then come inside and start writing again.

TO LEARN TO BE ALONE

P ASCAL'S GOT IT right I think. People get into trouble because they are unable to stay in their rooms. Pascal stayed in his and recorded his thoughts about our mortal state and also invented a geometric system or two. But Pascal was the exception and knew it. (Did he spend some time in a hair shirt? Highly possible.) Pascal—who did not think much of humanity; he called a man a thinking reed—was wary of the mischief we could get into when we worked our way through the locks and inserted ourselves into the outside world. So he stayed home and slept in his narrow bed and asked nothing of his servants and thought his usually rather chilling thoughts.

Pascal got things done. He did not leave his room. But not leaving one's room is a peril, as bad as being reviewed—as bad as the third glass can be. Though staying locked down inside has a few sweet pleasures, too.

I'm sure Pascal was abetted in his stay-at-home ways by his proclivity for writing. When you are isolated inside your room, you need something to do. Pascal, like every other writer, had to acquire the art of being alone. It's a good art to acquire and it's not terribly easy.

Everyone knows that a writer is a self-sentenced prisoner. For a certain part of every day, he must repair to a small walled enclosure. Whether it's a room of his own or rented from someone else is beside the point. There he is and there he stays. For a while, I wrote in a large, book-lined ship's-cabin-like structure. It was freestanding; it was rustic; it was full of books growing dusty and plants growing hardly at all, since plants must be watered and this was beyond the scope of the prisoner. But still, there was a certain rude luxury about the place. I had a music system to turn on and to juice myself with when inspiration failed. I was especially prone to listening to the live record by Dylan and the Band: *Before the Flood*. ("But time will tell just who has fell and who's been left behind / When you go your way and I go mine.") That amped me up pretty good. In grad school I lived in an apartment that was smaller by half than the place where I ended up writing my first books. In my studio, I had bay windows, I had wood floors, and after a while I had a bathroom. There was a bed I could conk out on and sometimes did. For a while a belief persisted among my sons that a horrible grouchy old man lived there. Then they found it was only their dad, and visited quite regularly.

Visiting too were friends who stopped by to say hello. All of them wished me well in my writing ventures; almost all of them mooned over my writing space. If only I had this, they said. If only I had this superb cabin of my own, then I would write. (Everyone it sometimes seems wants to write.) Then, truly I would be happy.

I like having friends. And since I like having friends, I did not let go of the words that were pushing against my lips with the force of souls trying to escape torment. Sure, I wanted to say: On Day One, you'd love it here. You'd put on some tunes, sharpen a few pencils, get a cup of coffee that's exactly right. You'd settle in in three bears style. You'd kick it all off with a little meditation, maybe Buddhist style, maybe the kind you learned at that workshop where they gave you a personal mantra in a quiet initiation ceremony. One more sip of the delectable brew and you'd sit down and begin to write. *Scratch, scratch/scrape, scrape.*

And by about noon, either that day or the next or the next, you'd be in the process of becoming a wreck. Not because you're dumb, not because you have nothing to say, not because you aren't "serious about writing." But because you, public persona, people person, rooster on the collective roost, have little experience in being alone. To write, you have to be able to countenance your own company. To write, you've got to be able to hang by yourself. You've got to go azul azul, as the Italian has it—or at least the improvised Italian that was spoken in the Hillside section of Medford, when I drank Bud and white port there with various and sundry, including Bova and Scialoia, and Castle and Carbone, circa 1971.

People can't stand themselves. They get all alone and they freak. They make a phone call, check their e-mails, click on the flat screen. In a pinch, they're even willing to pick up a book. But if you ask someone who has no experience in the game to write, even if you send him to his writing-room heaven, he's probably going to have a rough time. I surely did. I looked around my studio and saw that it was all I'd ever wanted as a writing hideaway and set to work. But then—an hour later, two at the most—I'd be itching for action, itching for people. I'd be out and in my car and on my way to town. Like most aspiring writers, I hadn't acquired the basic art. I hadn't learned the power that writing both relies upon and in the long run teaches. I did not know how to be alone.

I bored myself. That's the long and the short of it. And so does most every gal or guy who sits down to write. With all of his hustling in the world, he has only learned to use his mind as an instrument for success and the fulfillment of his desires. He has not learned to reflect and consider. When left alone, without anyone to talk to, he does not know what to do or say. He panics. And pretty soon the writing vocation or avocation that he's both affected to envy and made a little fun of begins to look daunting. After a week in the little room, it begins to look downright frightening. He will do anything to get out.

Adam was alone in the garden and smarted keenly about it. In Milton's rendering, he spends more than a little time petitioning God to bring him a partner, mate, and confidante. God seems to be in a bit of a playful mood (rare for Milton's God), and he teases Adam about his neediness. Look, I've made a paradise for you. What more could you want? Then God comes to his main point. Look at me. I have been alone here all through eternity and I'm not pining for release. Adam points out the gap that divides him from the Lord on high and God relents. When Adam is asleep, the Lord pulls a rib from Adam's side and fashions Eve. Then there's bliss, at least for a while.

But the point shouldn't be lost on us: there is something a touch godlike in the capacity to be alone. Of course we humans can usually only achieve a small-time version of the state. We're not alone for eternity as writers, but simply for two or four or six hours a day. Still, for us this is a feat. (Aristotle said that only a god or a beast could live entirely by himself.) And for others who are not adept in the art, it's rather undoable.

For to be alone, you have to be able to put up with yourself. Not for nothing does Jonathan Franzen suggest a challenge when he titles his book of essays *How to Be Alone*. Being alone is a skill. You've got to able to move your mind away from worry and obsession and plain noodling and focus on what's in front of you. You have to focus on what's before you, and that may be an empty page. But it also might be a gutter running with rainwater, a bird feeder alive with hyperactive wings and beaks, or a winter sky about to go into tantrum mode. You've got to able to be where you are and not with any intense alpha wave, front-of-the-brain intensity, but rather in a loose, easy, appreciative way letting what will come, come and enjoying it as it does.

The condition that exists when you write a leisurely first draft might well be an apt model for the best condition of consciousness in us all. Take it easy, as we used to say down at the Hillside park between pulls from the brown-bagged bottles and cans. Take it easy, but take it. Writing demands, from many, from most, a soft, easily suspended attention that is both alert and receptive. Receptive: Whatever comes, comes. Let's look and let's see. Alert: You've got to have your eyes open. You need something like an internal road map, though it's not good to peek at it too often. You have to be sharp but drifty and a little dull at the same time. You've got to receive and also to impart.

One of the most useful instructions a yoga teacher ever gave me was to cut the energy coming out of my eyes by about half. He had the right guy on this. I'm a practitioner of what feminists used to call the male gaze, though it's a touch more complicated than they say it is. I like to look at beautiful women, sure. But I also just like to look, stare, burn a hole in almost anything that's in front of me. Writing, for me at least, is way more compatible with the state in which you let it happen and let it flow. And that mode in turn—half in the game, half out of it—helps you to be alone in life. Or so I learned after a lot of false starts—a lot of sitting down at the computer, then running to the car and into town for an espresso and a chat.

When we're by ourselves our minds can get too busy. We think and rethink. We overprepare the event. We obsess on what will happen and might happen and could happen. Writing, with its relaxed focus on what is in front of you, and its combination of interest and receptivity to what's there, helps you to create the habit of mind that will let you be alone without the anxious semi-freak-out we sometimes suffer when we close the door behind us.

Presence: That's the habit of mind I think writing helps develop. It's a soft discipline that lets you be where you are—both when you're actually writing and when you're not. We humans are cursed (and I suppose blessed) by our knowledge of the future. Unlike the animals, we know the future actually will *exist*. So we're always on the lookout for what's coming—and not without reason. We're all looking ahead to old age and sickness and death. It's no easy trick to take your eye off the fiery ball that's coming our way and live in the present. In this pursuit writing can help, at least a little.

To be alone, you have to able to stand yourself. To stand yourself, well that requires the ability to soften and aim your mind. Writing helps you to do that. It's like a physical exercise that's salubrious in itself, and then pays you again and again as you go about your daily business.

The first days of being alone as a writer are tough. But you want to know yourself, you want to strengthen your mind, you want to learn to remember. (You may still also want to get rich and get famous and get the girl or the guy. But I'm betting those things will pass.) And so you begin the discipline of being alone, which ends up in time being something you need. As for myself, I need four to six hours of time azul azul in a given day and if I don't have them, I'll swipe 'em by staying up too late or getting up too early. I'm addicted to being alone, but that's better than being addicted to company. After all, I'm always there. And so are you.

TO READ AS A WRITER

ARE THERE ANY days that are better than the days of early reading? I mean the time, usually in youth, when you first fall in love with books. Every book is a fresh intoxication. Every author who matters to you (and there are so many!) initiates you into a vivid, unbroken dream. Reading delivers you from your all-too-fixed position in space and time and takes you to a world elsewhere. It's a form of magic, isn't it? No matter where you are, almost no matter what's going on around you, you can leave and go to some other place that is richer, more complex, and stranger yet also somehow more your home.

Books can cast spells, especially for the young. Every writer who matters to you (so many, and more to come) is a generous Prospero. He fills the island with wonders. She conjures the aurora borealis in the sky. I remember the bliss I felt when I learned that Shakespeare had written more than the three or four great tragedies one studies in high school. There were dozens of plays left! And all of them were there waiting for me.

The experience of reading in youth is one of total immersion. You become one with the author. You are no longer your ragged everyday self, but instead exchange minds and hearts with Walt Whitman or Nathaniel Hawthorne or Emily Dickinson. Suddenly our consciousness is expanded as we become identical if only for a while with a spirit larger than our own. We may not always be quite up to comprehending the splendors we encounter, but even in that sense of inadequacy there can be a feeling of optimism: There is more to learn, space to grow. There's more to being alive than I thought.

Reading early in life—or reading with the ardor of youth—is what we might even call a form of reincarnation. Suddenly, we are born again as another. We are reborn into a spirit larger and more intricate than the one we possessed.

We lose contact with our quotidian selves, and all our daily worries and desires swim back into the recesses. We are then other than we are—and we feel all the better for it. To read deeply when young is to see the world anew: to read, really read, while in the first phase of life is to be doubly young.

I remember the first time I picked up Thomas Wolfe's *Look Homeward, Angel*. What a revelation that book was for me. It was above all things a young man's book. Wolfe has a genius for rendering two drives in particular: ambition and desire. He is simply superb at chronicling what it is like to be young and to want to roll the world into a ball and have it as one's own to toss and catch as one might please. Desire: desire for sex and love and belonging; ambition: the urge to be the best, to do what hasn't been done, to be known and seen—no one could give that to you the way Wolfe could when he depicted Eugene Gant. No matter what Eugene was doing in the story, I somehow pictured his avatar behind him, legs spread, back arched, arms thrust upward to the sky, and crying out the words: "I want!" The emotions that fed the book were turbulent, but Wolfe gave you enough distance from them to look on with an assured tranquility. It was a serene dream of a beautiful, surging life, a life that might in time become one's own.

Was I indulging some wishes in reading this way? I probably was. But what's so wrong with indulging a few wishes, especially when you're young? Most people are conscious enough of wanting, often wanting in an aching sort of way. But what do they want? They frequently do not know. Part of reading when you're young involves putting yourself in touch with your desires. You identify with the protagonist, and what she wants you want, too. And so in her hopes, and the sorrows she goes through to fulfill them (or maybe to modify them or even to cast them aside), you shine a light down your future life.

But mostly I think early reading makes and elaborates a more general discovery and it is simply this: There is more to life than we had ever dreamed before. There is more to know and enjoy and fear and experience. And there is more—far more—to understand especially about the lives of others than we had ever thought. Safe within the mediated world of words we explore at a distance that is not too far and not too near the world as it can be. And we are enlarged—quietly but surely—by the experience.

Hypnotism, mild inebriation, dreaming, dropping into the preconscious mind: these are states we associate with early reading and they are wonderful. There is perhaps nothing like them in life. Sex can be what it can be, but it can never last as long as a good book can, no matter how slowly you proceed.

Early reading is wonderful. But if you're going to become a writer, you are going to have to stop doing it. You are going to have to take from yourself one of the great pleasures in your life. You're going to have to exchange a relatively easy pleasure for a far more difficult one. But isn't that a half-decent defini-tion of what growth entails? Exchanging easy for difficult pleasures?

When writers want to lose themselves in a vivid continuous dream, I think they usually go to the movies. No doubt a few have sustained the power to read like boys and read like girls, as some have sustained the power to do what Wolfe said you never could do: go home again. But not many.

What do writers read for? Many reasons, I suppose. But surely there is always a tutorial going on when a writer reads, especially when it's work in her own genre.

How did he do that? How did he make that happen? Can you really get away with that? Another narrator, this far into the book? Can she really bring that off?

At a certain point writers read a little the way pro ball scouts watch a game. There's pleasure and often admiration, sure. But there's also constant evaluation. Can he hit a curve? Can he throw a guy out from the warning track? Can he beat out an infield hit? But the scout is only compiling information. The writer drafts an internal report and then puts it to use for herself. She wants to learn what she can. Maybe she even wants to steal what she can. Good writers borrow, Eliot said. It is the great ones who manage to steal. (And, one might add, who manage to get away with it.) Writers read with their eyes wide open. Writers read to make a grab and then run off with what they have captured.

There is also the matter of competitiveness. Norman Mailer swore he never read novels when he was attempting to write one. He said it was as though he was out in his driveway repairing his car. There are parts scattered on the tarmac and even on the lawn. There's grease on his hands and there's grease on his pants. There's even grease on the grass. Then from the corner of his eye he catches a mint roadster, tuned to perfection, purring just right, and turning the corner like a cat. That's bad for morale. That's bad for the spirit. Avoid looking at that slick set of wheels. Get in the garage and go to work. Get in the garage, close the door, and stay there until you're done.

Mailer says that when he finished his own novel, he turned to the stack of his friends' books that had mounted up and up, and he read with a level of pleasure—and a level of generosity—that he savored. Maybe then he read as he did as a kid—swimming in James T. Farrell and John Dos Passos—if only for a day or two. But most of the time, he stayed in the garage.

He has a new book out! He does! He just published a book! Where did this one come from!

Writers, I fear, utter such words—if only under their breaths, or beneath the searchlight of their direct awareness—when they pick up the *Times Book Review*. And sometimes, if they're feeling wounded or pernicious, they turn a few pages or click the cursor and slide their eyes down to the final paragraph, hoping to see a little fire and brimstone rained down on the fellow too-fast author who up to this point they rather believed they liked. But no—it's a good review, a better than good one. Off goes a quick congratulatory note. (Easy to do with e-mail.) Now it's time to hunker down and get something of one's own done. Will our writer read his friend's just-trumpeted masterpiece? Not very likely. Not likely at all.

I have a writer friend who simply will not read Jonathan Franzen's novel *The Corrections* or, dammit, *Freedom* either. Though I think my friend would prefer to take up *Freedom*, being that he understands it to be a less accomplished book. You see there is not only reading as a writer, which is perilous. There is also not reading as a writer, which is perilous as well.

But why does my friend boycott Franzen? He does it for something of the same reason that Freud boycotted Nietzsche. Freud's rationale had been boiled down by Samuel Weber to a simple sentence: I will not read Nietzsche; I know he will be far too interesting. This writer does not read Franzen because he fears that Franzen might be far too good. He fears that Franzen might be a writer who has squared the circle: written good books (my friend has written good books) while at the same time writing books that sell (my friend's books have not really sold). Franzen's books can be real, if flawed, pleasures. (What novels are not flawed?) And my writer friend deprives himself of a genuine bounty by boycotting a fellow writer for (potentially) being too good and too interesting.

This may not happen to you, when you turn from reading to writing. One of the major themes of the book is the need to work against the inevitable dangers of writing and the writing life—envy, anger, the hunger for revenge, the desire for fame and wealth and copious untethered sex. But envy is a major pitfall. You can't be envious of the writer at hand and live fully in the world of his vivid and continuous dream.

In one of my favorite books, unread by almost everyone, a woman named Ann Marlowe uses her ten-year engagement with heroin to brood not only on drugs, but also on sex and music and time and anxiety and family and philosophy. Though her first time trying heroin could have killed her—she snorted too much—she says that she has never felt bliss in her life anything like it. All of the anxiety in her body and mind melted, and it was only then that she saw how much anxiety she had locked down like poisoning kryptonite in herself. She rose above time. She stopped time. (Thus the title of her book: *How to Stop Time: Heroin from A to Z*.) She loved it.

And then, not surprisingly, she went out to try to find that feeling again. No matter how many times she snorted dope, she never quite did it. The only paradises are lost paradises she came to think, and in time she stopped doing drugs. But she spent a decade looking for the lost paradise of the first time with the drug. "Ah," she says, "for the time when heroin felt instantly, overwhelmingly wonderful. If I had to offer up a one-sentence definition of addiction, I'd call it a form of mourning for the irrecoverable glories of the first time."

I've never done heroin, though there was a time when I was interested. When I worked at rock shows in the seventies, it was around but it never quite came my way. But when I think of times I have felt like a voyager in lotusland, void completely of anxiety, I think of my early days of reading. When Thomas De Quincey depicts his idea of terrestrial nirvana, he includes a snug room, a fire, a soft chair, snowflakes dropping like tiny white angels from the sky, and a book, a good book. Needless to say opium is involved, too. Reading and opium, it's said, go well together and it is no surprise. Says De Quincey: "Opium always seems to compose what had been agitated and to concentrate what had been distracted." Sounds a lot like reading, early reading.

And it's not surprising that people pursue the paradise of early reading with all of their might. I still do. I take home half a dozen books from the bookstore and library almost every weekend, hoping that one of them will cast the perfect spell. And sometimes, sometimes, it happens. I don't leave the couch. I forget to eat. I stay up half the night. Novels tend to do this for me, when it *is* done. Smith Henderson's *Fourth of July Creek* made it happen not long ago. But it's rare, rare. And then when it does happen, I go running off trying to find another dose and usually, of course, it doesn't work so well. As Marlowe says (though she's not talking about reading, not quite): "Yes, once in a while there's a night when you get exactly where you're trying to go. Magic. Then you chase that memory for a month. But precisely because you so want to get there it becomes harder and harder. Your mind starts playing tricks on you. Scrutinizing the high, it weakens."

Perhaps most people eventually find themselves exiled from the paradise of reading whether they become writers or not. They become too enmeshed in the world and its doings to be lost in the bliss of a perfect story or an exquisite poem. Or they go too often to the enchanted spring, the way Marlowe went too often to her drug, and they look to recapture an un-recapturable past, if they can.

But committing yourself to the life of writing is almost certain to drop you from regular access to the paradise of reading. You may be able to overcome your competitive envy. (I hope you can. I hope my friend will. He'd love Franzen.) But you'll probably never be able to overcome the detachment that being a practitioner entails. When a magician sits in the audience and watches the Houdini of the moment, he really has no choice but to look for the slips and the slides and to figure out how it's done by keeping his eye off the most obvious ball.

No one loves being exiled from paradise. Eve and Adam took it hard indeed and it's been that way down through time. But as the angel told them, they'd be compelled henceforth to create a paradise within themselves, assuming they could. The angel even said that the inner paradise could be "happier far" than what they had possessed when they were garden dwellers.

The paradise the writer seeks when he's cast out of the paradise of early reading is the one that writing can provide. For ultimately the pleasure of real writing outstrips the perils and pains of casting yourself out from the world of hypnotic reading, beautiful as that world was. Now, perhaps, as a writer you are providing entrance to that beautiful world for someone else.

TO DO *SOMETHING*

ONE OF THE facts that's affirmed constantly in the history of writing (which probably bears some relation to the history of literature) is the odd affiliations writers have. Writers don't usually feel themselves to be the spiritual kin of doctors and lawyers and corporate chiefs. They don't tend to feel at home in a room full of dedicated professionals. Most writers don't care for insurance salesmen or car salesmen or real estate brokers. In an auditorium full of junior trainees for middle management positions (with plenty of potential to ascend) they are like plants on time-lapse film, wilting for lack of water. At the end of the first presentation they are parched; at the end of the second they are a clump of dismal brown.

Writers don't usually fit in; there's no denying that. They are often the ones who hung wraith-like in the corner at the high school dance watching and pining (and judging) and feeling all the while like they had an invisible wound somewhere in their midsections. But then, of course, they didn't do what others of their disposition tended to do, which was to run home or to skip dances from then on. No, they came and they watched and they ached and they cultivated their loneliness and they hated their loneliness, too. There's a story by Thomas Mann called *Tonio Kröger* and Tonio is the artist as a very young man. We see him at dance lessons watching the beautiful movements of a perfect blond girl ("blue-eyed, laughing Inge") and feeling uncontrollable admiration and desire. She hardly knows that Tonio exists. The girl who does know is a little fräulein who is "always falling down in the dances," Magdalena. "She understood him, she laughed or was serious in the right places; while Inge the fair, let him sit never so near her, seemed remote and estranged, his speech not being her speech."

Has there ever been a writer who was an equal half of the perfect blond couple? And even if the writer wasn't one who fell down in the dance, he surely feared being relegated to the society of the clumsy and the unfit. The writer is often an outsider, as much by his own volition as by the designs of others—who frequently do not notice him much at all. He is unfit for social life, but he often is unfit—or makes himself unfit—for almost every other form of life as well. He tends to think of himself as a loner and maybe an outlaw, as someone who knows the rules and despises them. As Keith Richards sings it: "Always took candy from strangers / Didn't want to get me no trade."

Keith's alienation may not apply to every writer term for term: maybe he does know how to hold on to a book; maybe he's been afforded a second chance and a third; maybe he's got a fancy degree with which to decorate his wall (though no writer would do such a thing). Yet he feels a kinship to the semi-outlaw life that the Stones like to squall about. He doesn't want to play the game. He isn't like Mom and Dad and Buddy and Sis.

And often, he doesn't become alienated because he is a

writer. He becomes a writer because he is alienated. Writing gives him somewhere to go when he thought there was nowhere. Despite perils, writing manages to give him some pleasure in a life he thought would be mostly pain.

He may have no early interest in language or getting matters down on paper. He's probably a reader—all half-decent writers are. But it may be—it often is—that a writer turns to writing because he's not capable of doing anything else.

This was surely the case with Henry Miller, who didn't turn to writing until he was about forty and had screwed up every other endeavor he'd undertaken. He was, he attests, horrible at business, a miserable husband, a wash as a son, even a crummy friend if you wanted to know the truth. (Don't leave your wife alone with Hen.) Miller went off to Paris not mainly to be an artist but because he could live the vagabond's life more cheaply there.

If there is any vocation with which writers have an affinity, it is probably that of the vagabond. When a writer sees a traveling hobo, a rambling guy with a guitar in a cardboard box, a street singer roving from town to town, he feels immediate kinship and at least a dram of admiration. Here is someone who has taken it all the way. He couldn't find anything to do in this futile, ridiculous world either. But rather than stopping at the last step before the cliff—I'm a writer, a writer!—he stepped directly over and went into free fall. A writer has just enough anxiety in him about what other people think and just enough fear of radical and prolonged discomfort not to make the final move, pack his comb and harmonica in a handkerchief, tie it to a stick, sling the stick over his shoulder, and begin rambling off to the beat of an endlessly looping Hank Williams song.

Now granted there are middle-class writers who want all the

comforts and speak about writing as a profession and themselves as practitioners of a noble calling. These are women and men who can have dinner with a table full of rich bankers and businessmen and listen to their pompous opinions (they must be smart; they are rich) and not fall out of their chairs laughing at their self-importance and servitude to riotous jargon. Such writers exist and they write novels about the suburbs and live in the suburbs on occasion, too. They want to be normal and they try to be nice. By and large it doesn't work and they pay for it.

Real writers are at least in some measure outcasts. They are wandering Jews—and wandering Christians and Muslims and nonbelievers, too. They can't fit and they can't do what they are supposed to do. They don't always fall down in the dance, but often they can't stand the music. So why do they have to express their sorrows? Why can't they just shut up about it—like most of the other pariahs of the world do?

The question is not an easy one. Why must they make a record of their own and wave their hands at the world: Look at me! Listen! Here's my book! I hate you all! Why do this when the writer's initial feeling about the human world, the social world, is often one of at least partial rejection? Why not simply roll with it?

Perhaps writers who write from the edges are trying to compound an explanation. And what they are trying to explain is nothing so much as themselves. They wish to explain themselves to themselves. Why am I as I am? Why always in the corner? Why will none of the common pursuits do for me? Is it sheer vanity that makes me this way? Is it stubbornness? Is it at bottom a fear, a fear that if I really did immerse myself in the game of life I would be one of the hard-trying losers? Every lyric poet and almost every essayist and a few novelists and story writers to boot pose these impossible-possible questions to themselves. These are the questions that Montaigne asked himself and Proust, but also the questions of Emerson and Thoreau and Dickinson and Whitman. ("I and this mystery here we stand," Whitman says.) It is also the question of ragtag bobtail writers all down through the centuries.

But then why publish the results to the world? You could just as well lock your journal and toss the key, or declare to yourself that it is not for nothing that "essay" means "attempt" and that trying to make permanent what was meant to be transitional and notation is forcing the issue.

Writers often publish out of vanity, vanity and the desire for a dollar. But an author can be generous, too. A writer can mean well not only for himself but for others. He knows there are many people like the self he once was (and continues in certain ways to be). There is no end of people equally confused and lonely and distressed and looking to understand why this is and if it truly must be. It is simple humane generosity that makes certain kinds of outcasts writers. They write, as the great outcast Socrates told them to, in order to know themselves. But they also write to open the doors of understanding to others—and especially the young, who stand outside.

People surprise themselves all of the time. People shock themselves all of the time, especially when they are young. They think thoughts, feel feelings, experience impulses that are radically strange, and when they do they ask the inevitable questions: Am I alone? Am I some sort of freak, some sort of monster? Has anyone ever felt this way before?

But then they find writers who can unlock their isolation for them. They're sprung from the prison cell of self. They see that the world is more complex and varied and strange than they had imagined; in fact the world is as complex and varied and strange as they are themselves. They see there are others like them who don't believe the commonplace and can't stand the hype and the cant and the jive. These people are writers, very often.

As puerile as the Beats can sometimes seem to me now, when I read them at the age of seventeen or so they were deliverance. Jack Kerouac had one dream, one aspiration above all the others. He wanted to get the hell out of here. Nothing pleased him about stable life; nothing made him happy on Main Street, with the people passing and greeting their everyday greetings and sighing their everyday sighs. He wanted out. He was only happy when he was on the road and on the move, listening to the chants of his manic friend Neal Cassady. The only freedom was in motion. No one ever read *On the Road* all the way through without wanting to take to the highway. No one ever read the book with sympathy without seeing the trudging life around him with new eyes, and with more confident eyes. To do the same thing every day in the same place! Wasn't this hiding from life?

Kerouac saw that habit and routine and repeating, repeating, repeating were dumb counterspells. They were ways to pretend that time wasn't passing. We could think today was yesterday and both would be tomorrow. We warded off thoughts of death and change but did so at the expense of dulling of the spirit. We got grayer and more tired in our timidity. America, maybe, was getting grayer and more tired in its timidity. So Kerouac and his pals—silly, charming, bumptious, sly, occasionally smart—took off for the territories. Their only pleasure came in movement. "Power ceases in the instant of repose," says Emerson. Power is in movement; power is in transition. "It resides in the moment of transition from the past to a new state, in the shooting of the gulf, in the darting to an aim."

Then the sage adds a critical perception. "This one fact the world hates, that the soul becomes." The world hates the people who try to change for the better. It hates the people who remind it that it has grown stale and old and is now in the habit of congratulating itself for doing so. The world came to hate Kerouac in time. No writer in my memory was so roundly mocked. And he did not take it well. He turned up on TV drunk and slurring; he insulted his enemies or those he imagined would be his enemies if he gave them half a chance. But he had his reasons. "It's not writing, but typing," they said of *On the Road.* Tell that to a generation of kids, me included, that the book shook out of dull sleep. We loved that book then and in my experience students and young people of all sorts have continued to love it for over fifty years.

But Kerouac paid the price for what I have to see as his generosity. He was a working-class kid from Lowell and he was an athlete, a star football player. Yet he had the heart of a poet. Ginsberg says he learned more about poetry from Kerouac's short lyrics than he did from any of his contemporaries. Allowances made for friendship: this is still no small accolade. But Kerouac had too many internal tensions to stand up to the abuse he took. He crumpled and drank some; got hit, crumpled, came back, wrote more, and drank some more. He wrote with the kind of fury that someone who is being chased by ridicule and can't stand it must often do.

I suppose Kerouac may have wanted many of the conventional rewards writers strive for. I'm sure he wanted to make a dollar and see his name in the paper—though once one has seen one's name in the paper in a certain manner, it is a wish that declines. But I also think that he—lonely in himself, and writing out of a protracted loneliness—wrote for all the other isolates and brilliant sad cases that dotted America. What a godsend to me and my friends he was. He was born only a few miles away from us and he lived in Lowell, Massachusetts. Lowell! A city we cruised to on Saturday nights to hear rock bands and drink and maybe pick a fight. Kerouac lived a twenty-minute car ride from our two- and three-decker houses. Kerouac!

He got himself in trouble at Columbia. Though he was a terrific student and a fine athlete he consorted with bums and ne'er do wells. He even let Allen Ginsberg sleep over! And he sent his writing out to us. Even excoriated by those who were supposed to know—not writing, but typing—he kept at it, telling us things about what we could do to break out. Travel? Sure, of course. But there's nature and the mountain climb. There's Zen. There's the holy spirit of jazz. There's the kind of friendship that's about more than networking and small-timing it to the top. I think Kerouac was a generous writer. I think many writers are generous writers.

He wouldn't have lasted a minute with those great lawyers Dylan talks about, discussing lepers and crooks. He wasn't management material. He was one of nature's warmhearted vagrants. He ended up a sad overweight drunk, living with his mother back in Lowell. And this in some part was because he reached out to the other lost souls in America and they heard him. None of the professors liked his books—not the way they did F. Scott Fitzgerald's anyhow—and they let him know about it.

Kerouac wrote because there was probably nothing else he could do in this world and he wanted to figure out why that was. And he wanted others who were in the same fix to breathe a little easier and feel a bit more at home in America. If they didn't like what they saw around them, they could always take a ride. I hope that on some level, despite the sorrows, Kerouac from time to time took some pleasure from what he'd done for us. It's a pleasure all writers can aspire to, though the pains attendant are real enough.

TO HOLD YOUR PEACE

HAS THE WORLD always been as full of talkers as it is now? I can't imagine it has. We would have had more testimony down through time about the plague of chatterboxes that was besetting the human race—filling the air with their clamor, polluting all public space and most private, and drowning out the music of the spheres. Alexander Pope seems to write about a comparable situation in *The Dunciad*. But so gifted and to the point was Pope that almost anyone outside himself and his esteemed circle of friends (Swift and Arbuthnot and the rest) might seem a clamoring dope. Plutarch wrote an essay on nonstop-talking bores. Yet it is, rather shockingly for that fascinating writer, a bit of a bore itself.

No, the plague of yackers that besets us seems to be something of a current phenomenon. It is, maybe, a sign of our era. Everywhere you go, people seem to be pinning others, often (nominally) their friends, to the mat and having at them with words. Listeners are tied to the track and run over with nonstop discourse. What is a dinner party now but a site where all the alphas present (and everyone now aspires to alpha status) vie for the position of king of the oratorical hill? This status is usually achieved not by being the most articulate, the most learned, or the most original. It is achieved by being the loudest, the most aggressive, and the least sensitive to the desires of others to be—every hour or so and ever so softly—heard. But there is an upside to this. At least there is for the writer: you can convert this pain to pleasure. You can take it from gap to gain.

True to the spirit of the original child's game, the grown child who seeks to be king of the oratorical hill pushes other aspirants down by talking more—and more loudly—than anyone else. He goes on and on and on. Challenge him and he raises his tone higher until it sounds like he is bellowing in a church. Or he resorts to subtler stratagem to hold the floor. I have witnessed a man make adept use of his stutter to call attention to himself, to incite sympathy and thus silence, and then to take over the dinner table like a mutineer captain taking over shipboard.

Is it necessary to say that the most common dinner-table mutineer captains are male? A woman may do it from time to time, but it seems often a political gesture, a drive for equality, or an object lesson to show the males around the watering hole exactly what it's like. But usually the orator is phallic.

There is, from what I can tell, a genre of book that aids and abets this practice. Such books are found in airports and often composed by contributors to various glossy magazines. They tell you how the stock market really works, why there is so much poverty in America, what the next wave of computers will be like, what's hot in real estate, and why in football the left tackle means as much as he does. From what I can tell, males buy these on the way home from business trips, skim them on the plane, arrive home at six, and by eight thirty, fork in one hand knife in the other, are regaling a set of relative innocents with a summary of the book's contents. Often they do not cite the author. They claim, implicitly, that this knowledge has been compiled by none other than themselves. They never shut up. In small cities, the table toppers may often use *New York Times* articles to hold the fort; in big cities it seems only a book will do.

These usurpers are, as I say, most often male. I have heard a story about a young woman who put up with one of these dinner party disquisitions for as long as she could stand it. But this time the perp actually named the book he was citing—a breakthrough for him no doubt. She informed him quite directly that she knew the book well. She had read it multiple times. He continued talking. She knew the book she claimed inside and out. On the elocutionist went. This was a book, she averred, from which she could quote freely. Didn't stop the dude. She then declared to him and all others listening that she had in fact *written* the book.

The orator took this in. He contemplated the fact. He did not doubt her. After a decorous pause, he spoke again. He took up where he left off, explaining the author's book to her and all others who could bear to listen. Now I'm not sure I believe this one out and out. But let it stand as an emblem for the current discursive situation in certain provinces of American culture.

The urge to orate is not limited to dinner tables at present. It is everywhere and it is not easy to account for. If Tocqueville were to come back from his aristocratic grave in France and tour America once more, he might well tell us that it all owed to the factor that the author of *Democracy in America* believed explained most of what mattered in the states— the rule of the people. Sometimes Tocqueville thought that the rule of the people, democracy, brought you uncomfortably close to anarchy. So why does everyone want to talk? Maybe because he who speaks is king, or at least rules for the present. If nobody rules, maybe anybody can. As Springsteen says, "Poor man wanna be rich / Rich man wanna be king / King ain't satisfied 'til he rules everything." So everybody wants to hold the floor. And I mean everybody. I've listened to interminable monologues by people still residing deep in their teens about their (brief) lives and (thinly perceived) times. At discourse's end, they inquire to know what my name might be so they can send me a daily chorus of tweets. Tocqueville warned me. I didn't listen. George Steiner wrote the essay "The Distribution of Discourse" in which he bemoaned the passage from the day when Dad talked a lot and Mom talked a little, but to potent effect—and everyone else simply jammed a fist between his teeth and listened.

There's also, I think, the self-justifying business. Again, it has to do with democracy, a little. To wit: no one knows anything. No one knows with certainty what's good or bad, right or wrong in the way of the conduct of life. Sure there are laws. Sure there are mores, even a few manners. But people often feel uncomfortably like they are making it all up as they go along. Am I who I say I am? Am I living the right way? Does my life make sense? In the current random, these questions can feel up for grabs.

A lot of what the yackers do in my experience is to justify the peculiar and often rather contingent forms their lives have taken. They are not only telling you, and the rest of the unfortunates standing by with the ice melting in their drinks, who they are. They are telling themselves. When there are not a lot of templates out there, when the Ten Commandments could be nine or four, but probably not fourteen or thirty, it's hard to figure out who one is and why that matters. Did Mailer write a book called *Advertisements for Myself*? In our time it seems everyone is advertising for himself. Everyone needs the microphone, everyone needs the floor, everyone is perpetually clearing his throat to set in, and once in he will not conclude until the Dog Star rages (which, I gather from Lord Byron, is quite a long time). The era of the orator is upon us. Everyone wants to be a (relatively benign) dictator—which, as Northrop Frye reminds us, is nothing other than a speaking machine—a nonstop talker.

It's no pleasure spending one's life as an ongoing audience. When one of the self-justifiers or front-table monarchs is rattling down the tracks like an empty train with all its couplings loose, you feel crummy. There's something diminishing about having someone let loose a monologue in your face. You can feel your sense of self shrink a little with every fresh dependent clause. The candle flame of ego begins to splutter. How long before it winks completely out? That's what the talker wants, naturally. They grow and you shrink. It's a zero-sum activity. Has anyone ever spoken of castration by conversation?

But. However. Consider.

Once you've gone over and become a writer, at least in your own mind, all of this changes. And the purgatory of eternal listening can become something like a pleasure. Now you know that after the storm of discourse is over, you can go back to the room of your own, or to your corner of the coffee shop, and set the truth down as you see it. You can write and rewrite and compose and recompose, and indulge in all the necessary visions and revisions, and have yourself some latte or some hot chocolate while you're there. In other words, you will get your turn.

Now this may be small comfort to some, but there is more. While being regaled you can stop feeling that you are suffering in silence and realize a critical truth. You are not a passive victim any longer. You are in the role of God's spy. Whether you write poems or novels or plays or blog posts, you are gathering material. This will be of use. This will pay off.

My wife, the most socially kind person I know, endorses listening to bores with rapt attention. She finds it to be an exercise in Zen self-effacement—good for the modesty, good for the soul. But she is also always on the watch for a fine phrase— fine because it's artful or (more often) fine because it illuminates a certain personality to perfection. This fine phrase will reappear in an arch short story of hers somewhere down the line. And so will the phrase's—I was going to say originator. But often the speaker is simply channeling the latest in some form of pop patois: medical, political, environmental, what have you. And the speaker may turn up in her story, too, though charitably disguised.

The final truth about the situation of the writer in the world of windbags is still yet unspoken. Ask Jane Austen about it—or ask her works. And there you will encounter what can only be highly civilized, exquisitely refined writer's reparation. (Which is something not quite like the wholesale kamikaze revenge I spoke of earlier.) I would eagerly bet that each and every prosing gasbag in *Pride and Prejudice* had a prototype in the realms of what people sometimes foolishly call Austen's "limited experience." I'm guessing that the bumptious social-climbing Mrs. Bennet had one; and that the insufferable parson, Mr. Collins, got his start on a pulpit not far from Ms. Austen; and the drably ferocious dragon, Lady Catherine de Bourgh, spent some time posing for Austen in some sublunary form before she made it into the celestial pages of the novel.

And then all the Mrs. Bennets and Lady Catherines and Mr. Collinses down through time had the pleasure of seeing themselves in the novel—or at least their associates did, since people like Mr. Collins and company are inclined to avoid anything resembling a mirror.

Revenge? Revenge is too strong a word. There is no poison in evidence, no dagger, not even a lawsuit with a well-buttoned advocate pleading one's case. But there is a measure of mild retribution and it has its savors. The writer may not get the first word at the dinner party, or many of the words that flow in the middle like bland lava. But if she's anything like Jane Austen, she can always get the last.

PLEASURES AND PERILS

TO LEARN SOMETHING

I HAVE BEEN a teacher now for thirty-five years and when people ask me why I love the job (which I do) I sometimes lie—or at least I leave the main motive out. I tell them how much I like students (and I do) and how much I love the feel of colleges (they often seem like ideal cities to me) and how well I get along with my colleagues (true, most all the time). But what I leave out is that I love teaching because it is the only way I've ever found to learn anything that mattered to me. When I want to know more about something—philosophy, religion, movies, books—I arrange to teach a course about it. I'm a passive reader (half the time I'm dreaming away) and when I go to a lecture I one-third listen at best. But when I have to give a lecture or present a class, the mental beams (such as they are) go on high (or as high as they get) and I actually learn what I am supposed to teach.

There are writers who write to learn not what they already know (on some level) but those who write to discover new aspects of the world outside themselves. (They write for much the same reason that I, and many others like me I'll bet, go into teaching: without what we taught ourselves teaching others, we'd be dopes.) I love writers who are perpetual students, the sorts of people who become hungrily curious about one thing or another and go to work to learn all they can about it. What they write for is to discover something new. The writing can almost be an *excuse* for the learning. A person suddenly becomes possessed by the idea of learning about gardening or fly fishing or architecture or the way Wall Street works (and doesn't) and then goes to work, chugging down facts and metabolizing them at a velocity that often leaves me stunned. I'm the archetypal slow learner and I'm pleased and grateful when a quick learner comes along and dives headfirst into a fascinating subject and acquires triple time what would take me years to capture, and then serves it all up in sterling silver prose. Such writers find pleasure themselves and yield it in no small measure to their readers.

Such writers tend to be optimists. They tend to love the world. Though they are often critics of what they consider (Wall Street!), they have an abiding faith that change will soon be tinting the horizon. "If winter comes," says the poet, "can spring be far behind?" They write slashing exposés like *Fast Food Nation* and they do hyper-overtime research and holler expertly at the banks. And then they pop up two or three years later working on some only partially related subject having gorged themselves again on facts, facts, and more facts. They are the servants of humanity and they are perpetual students.

Walter Benjamin says the correct attitude toward life (which means it is surely the correct attitude toward writing) is that of children in fairy tales—cheerful, confident, and resourceful, ready to take on whatever comes. Anyone who has read the Oz books (the movie is a slightly different matter) knows that

Dorothy is a wonder. Weird things are always happening to this American Alice in Wonderland, but unlike perpetually nonplussed Alice, the polite English girl, Dorothy is never taken completely by surprise and always knows what to do. She's curious, warm, and ready for anything, a perpetual student of the bizarre world of Oz. Writers who learn and teach are students of our own often Oz-like world of marvels and they often lack nothing of Dorothy's doughty spirit.

A certain sort of writer is a perpetual student. Writing is his excuse to educate himself. Where other men and women are satisfied to go off and read a book about the president or the latest war or the way we eat now, this kind of writer goes out and writes one. He travels and he reads and he interviews and he researches. He spends as much time away from his desk gathering materials as he does sitting down and composing the book. He's a sociable sort of person, the educating writer, and he has the very rare capacity of being equally at home with people and at his desk. Hannah Arendt said that to be a politician you had to be able to spend protracted periods of time with people you fundamentally do not like. Many writers—I'd even say most—don't like much of anyone and live a sort of self-imposed internal exile. This kind of writer, the writer who writes to learn and teach, has a gift for liking everyone, or at least everyone who can help him enlarge his base of knowledge. He can cruise a cocktail party to find the staffer who'll tell him what's up in Congress, or cold-call a scientist to learn all about nuclear fission (or fusion), but then he can repair to his home, turn off the phone, recede from the Internet, and get working. Unlike other writers, who often spend the three hours of a dinner party watching their hands, the educating writer can chat nimbly with all comers. Norman Mailer saw this quality in his contemporary Dwight Macdonald, who, Mailer said, could immerse himself in deep discourse with an Eskimo making his first visit from the tundra within five minutes of being introduced. Most sociable people can't write; most writers can't schmooze. This kind does both.

The persona of the student is one of the most attractive of human identities and one of the most pleasure yielding. Not only does it often yield much-praised literary results, but it also feels good to inhabit. You can roll through life like a feisty cub, asking questions, smiling, and doing the dance of deference, which people naturally love you for. You can be a terrific listener because a little like old Rumpelstiltskin, you'll soon be spinning the conversational straw into gold. People love to hold forth, especially insecure intellectual types, *male* types in particular. And there you are to catch their words in a pearl basin. Then back to the office and the desk and the Herman Miller Aeron Chair to kick back and put it all in order.

The persona of writer-student doesn't only work well in the research phase. People love to hang out with a literary learner. That's what reading his books can feel like—hanging out with him or her. He doesn't make them insecure or nervous. He doesn't make them feel dumb, the way old-time writers like Milton and Spenser do. If anything, readers maybe feel a bit sharper than he is. He is so earnest, so modest, so solicitous of their attention, and so determined to feed them the material in tasty (and nutritious) bites. He puts himself in the readers' place and asks all the questions they want to ask; he anticipates their feelings and addresses them in humane, nonstuffy ways. He writes profiles and features for the *New Yorker* and bestselling books for every outlet that pays. What he does is hard to do, and the world thanks him (if he does it well) with coins by the chestful and trophies and plaques.

But the peril is this: the writer who writes to learn often doesn't write that well. He hasn't had time to metabolize his material, so he writes out of the front of his brain and not out of the feelings in his gut. He goes off and finds subjects, rather than letting subjects find him, bubbling up from the bottom of the cauldron that is his creative source. Yeats, very late in his career, says he's searching for a subject and can't find one, just can't. He pines and even grieves a bit, but he eventually comes to a solution. He's going to go back down to where all of his work has always begun: "the foul rag and bone shop of the heart." The business about his creative unconscious being foul seems to me to be simply Yeats's everyday being—his selfhood—talking. He doesn't want to descend into the mess of memories and dreams and fantasies. It's damned embarrassing. But Yeats, great poet that he is, knows that true subjects are in you and have to be dived down after—or simply waited for.

Writing a book or an article about something you get interested in for the purpose of writing a book or an article is often going to result in thin gruel. People may read the book once for the information, and the timely buzz. But they won't go back to it time after time. The best writers, I think, don't only want to be read; they want to be reread.

The late Christopher Hitchens was a writer who could take the events of the day—even a particularly brutal or strange day—and spin them into sense overnight. Hours after the attacks of 9/11, Hitchens was churning out reasonably astute, reasonably thoughtful reactions. And Hitchens could write a book in a trice. He blazed into a subject, got a grip on it, and produced something lively and smart. He attacked religion; he attacked Bill Clinton and Hillary; he even went after Mother Teresa. He savaged Lord Elgin for stealing the marbles from the Parthenon. Hitch's fires flared brightly, but they were often fed by paper and sticks. Try rereading any one of these books and you'll see how glib they are. One feels he is in the hands of a man who wants to make his word count for the day, have a drink, and get paid. I loved Hitchens the journalist. When something of note happened, he was the one I wanted to read first. I just didn't want to read it again the next day. Hitchens was a teacher and Hitchens was a student—glad to learn, glad to teach. But even in his memoir, you can't say he wrote from the guts. That sort of thing just wasn't in him. He was in a major hurry, always running like Alice simply to stay in the same place.

Yet there are days when I—and I suppose many others— would trade a good deal to be this sort of student-writer. Such people have a connection with readers that one envies. They really do work for their constituency. They find the subjects that will interest the public; they go at them in a direct way; they answer all questions and leave nothing unsaid. They are like literary lawyers and doctors, performing a service the world seems to need—and for which the world sometimes rewards them munificently.

Do they ever *shape* taste, or expand consciousness? Not very likely. When they hear the poet say that the writer must create the taste by which he will be appreciated, they nod dismissively. They don't want to enlarge consciousness or question existing protocols of thought. They want to please and instruct, with the pleasing always coming first. They want their readers to feel hip, knowing, and at home in the world. They are all too often the equivalent of a warm blanket and a cup of tea, however insouciant they may pretend to be. And yet I have no doubt that without them the world of writing would be a far poorer place. Write to learn; write to teach. It brings pleasure (and yields pleasure), but it's got its perils, too. It's not the noblest way to butter one's toast I suppose, but it's far from the worst.

The midgame writer has to decide if he or she will go this route or not. Will she walk over the terrain of current culture with the equivalent of a divining rod, hoping to be drawn to the next big topic that's just slightly buried but ready to surface? Or should she follow her heart, and write what she most wants to write? That way has perils, too. One knows what it is like when your interests simply do not line up with the existing interests of the world at large. One has had the experience of composing the right book at the wrong time. But insofar as you are free of the exigencies of your purse, I think it best to write about what you love, and leave the journalism, even the higher journalism, to the fast and the fluent, and those hoping to make the literary slot machine pay out with a hooting of whistles, a clanging of bells, and an avalanche of brass tokens. Love is hard to find—and harder as life goes on and one enters the middle distance. To be able to do something—anything—from the heart is a pleasure and a gift not to be denied.

TO STAY SANE

EVERYONE KNOWS THE line about how great wits are near to madness aligned. One might add that at times moderate and minor wits are, too. Hitchcock's Norman Bates mutters once that everybody goes a little mad sometimes, and in this, if nothing else, Norman is probably not far from the truth.

Writing is not likely to cure a haunting depression or a truly torturing case of anxiety and as for the more serious psychological maladies—schizophrenia, bipolar disorder and the like—writing will do no more for the suffering soul than persistent whistling would. But I think for many of us who want to retain sanity—keep our balance, stay in the game—writing is not a half-bad form of therapy. I'm not talking about writing at length about one's sorrows and sufferings. I'm not thinking about writing as a mode of defining one's inner maladies. But I do think the habit of writing can help many people in the quest to be reasonably balanced on an emotional or—why not say it?—a spiritual level. And sanity—what greater pleasure is there than that, especially when one contemplates the alternatives, or has experienced them.

Harold Bloom says that the major trope used by American writers is the trope of surprise. They did not specialize in irony or metaphor, but in the surprising of others and themselves with what came forth on the page. It's not hard to imagine Walt Whitman waking in the morning after an evening's bout with the poem that would become *Song of Myself* (in its first manifestation it had no title). Reading over his efforts from the night and day before, Whitman couldn't but sigh and laugh a Broadway laugh and say something like: "I did that. I Walt Whitman wrote those words!"

For Whitman's arrival as a poet was to say the least surprising. He had no formal education; he knew no literary people; he had failed in almost everything he'd tried to do. (He'd flunked as a schoolmaster purportedly because he failed to beat the boys.) At the ages of thirty-one and thirty-two he had a heroically bad temperance novel to his credit (it was called *Franklin Evans*), a stint as editor of the *Brooklyn Eagle*, and some skill as a printer. He was working as a carpenter. No one expected much of anything—though on some level he surely did himself. When he began to write the entries in his notebook that would eventually become *Leaves of Grass*, he was framing two-room houses in Brooklyn.

What he wrote in that journal could only have surprised him. It still surprises most anyone who reads it now. In one entry that (probably for the better) doesn't make its way directly into the poem, Whitman imagined himself sauntering down the streets of heaven. Whitman never rushed, never trotted. He was always taking it slow, looking at what was around him, a saunterer extraordinaire. On the streets of heaven, Whitman sees Jahweh, Lord God of Hosts, deity of Abraham and Moses coming his way. Whitman is suddenly struck with a major perplexity. What's he going to do in regard to the hat issue? To wit: Is he going to tip his hat to Yahweh before Yahweh tips to him? (Yahweh wears a hat?) Is he going to show the Lord *that degree* of deference? For Walt Whitman is part of a singular species of being. He is, as he will say in the poem, "Walt Whitman, an American." At length, Whitman decides he'll tip his cap to the creator of the universe if the creator makes the gesture first, or at least signals willingness to bring off a simultaneous cap tip.

More than a decade later, during the Civil War, Whitman worked as a male nurse amid the wounded, both Union and Confederate, in Washington, D.C. On his morning walks, Whitman occasionally used to see the president of the United States, Abraham Lincoln, out alone taking the air. One wonders who was the first to touch his hat.

Whitman is playing a bit (one hopes) when he talks about meeting Yahweh in heaven and withholding deference. But how could he have imagined he would ever create such a scenario, even right up to the moment of composition. Even afterward, he must have been filled with surprise bordering on awe. I said that. I wrote that. Walt Whitman, an American, who turned out to be more than the son of Walter Whitman, the drunken Quaker carpenter who mistreated Walt and his brothers when they were growing up. Surprise.

Writing when it is going well is all about surprise. We laugh and sigh and whisper and look in a kind of awe at the strangeness of what we are occasionally moved to put on the page. Who is speaking when the voice we hear is both ours and not ours? Where do utterances like Walt Whitman's come from?

The answer perhaps is obvious. We are not one self but many. We teem with different voices, different attitudes, different founts of appreciation and judgment. In certain sorts of writing, we let these ancillary and antiselves get out and take the air. We let them strut and fret their hour on the stage and be heard in due measure.

Psychoanalysis teaches us that what is not available to consciousness abides in the realm of the repressed and is therefore toxic, pathological. The material that comes forth on the couch, in free association, rises from a personal Tartarus. It's a twisted and tormented discourse, infected with wayward desires. But writing suggests that that which is not present on the surface isn't necessarily pathological. We have voices in us, dreams and desires that have been banished or pushed to the rear not because they are poison. At their worst they are inconvenient. They don't help us get on with the day. They aren't practical. They don't help shake fruit from the tree or grind the wheat or ferment the wine. But they are waiting nonetheless. What they wait for is to be expressed and the expression I believe is healthful. It creates a higher sanity.

Psychoanalysis is right about this. Much is latent; much goes unsaid. And the pain of the unsaid is real. It makes for anxiety, too much needless buzz in the psyche. But what is unsaid is not always poison or harmful; it's not always a black acid rain that requires a therapist on hand to open an umbrella. Much of what lies unspoken, as Whitman's great poem shows, is benign or even benevolent, albeit sometimes rather peculiar.

In *Song of Myself* the poet travels through life like a demiurge: "I pass death with the dying and birth with the new washed babe and am not contained between my hat and boots." He shows up at a frontier wedding between a trapper and an Indian girl; he's there during what he calls an old-time sea-fight and also present at a massacre during the Mexican-American War.

He watches people doing their jobs—ploughmen and singers and bartenders and factory workers and carters and printers like himself. The list is almost endless. Whitman loves to watch people work—though one senses that concentrated physical labor is something the poet himself shies from a bit. He watches a well-bred woman watch twenty-eight handsome young men frolicking naked in the water. And then he watches her imagine jumping in with them and he becomes her (and gets to frolic with those young men himself). He watches animals and talks to them (in the way a child can do) and says at one point that he could happily go and live among them because as far as he can see they don't complain all the time or try to foist religions on each other. (Whitman likes everyone just about, minus priests and occasionally, alas for me, minus school-teachers.) He runs off with the runaway slave and feels the sting of the rifle ball as it penetrates his leg and he hears the yelp of the pursuing dogs.

As any reader of the poem will know, this is only a sampling of what Whitman does and sees. But if he is fascinated by the life of the world—and he is—he is also fascinated by the life of his spirit. "I and this mystery here we stand," says Whitman, and he's not kidding. His internal life is a mystery, though he intends to explore it and does before the poem finishes. Whitman isn't one person, unified and alone, far from it. Besides the being he shares with other Americans there is an interior being, too. "Apart from the pulling and hauling stands what I am," he says. This self, whom he calls the "Me-myself," is "amused, complacent, compassionating, idle, unitary . . . Both in and out of the game, and watching and wondering at it." Whitman's Me-myself is quite shy, sensitive, observant, neither male nor female—and in fact perhaps beyond the beckoning of desire. There is no precedent for such a being in any prominent map of the spirit before or after Whitman, at least none that I know about. Freud surely has no use for a Me-myself, and even devotees of Whitman, like Ginsberg and Crane, don't adopt the persona.

Through writing, Whitman discovers an as yet undisclosed aspect of himself and then deploys it to discover fresh qualities in the world. It is, we might think, the uncovering of the Me-myself that makes Whitman as patient and observant as he is. Part of what appeals about *Song of Myself* is its slow-motion indolence: the poet rambles and looks and ponders. He's never in a hurry. The Me-myself will not be rushed.

I think this opening up of the inner life was conducive to health and sanity for Whitman and I think similar opening can be good for almost all of us. What rises to the surface when Whitman expands himself through writing isn't usually forbidden material. His poetry isn't about the return of the repressed. It's about new discovery—new thresholds, new anatomies, as Hart Crane would say. It feels good to expand the mind and to get the results of that expansion into words and into the world.

By following Whitman and expressing what's latent inside we can give ourselves a marvelous sort of peace and tranquility. Freud was right when he said that putting thoughts and feelings into words brought peace. We only need to amend him to say the thoughts and feelings don't have to be of a forbidden nature. Simply to give expression to what is latent in us can be a source of calm joy. Wallace Stevens has a marvelous phrase that bears on this process. He talks about "the hum of thoughts evaded in the mind." By giving expression to those thoughts, the evasions stop. And the hum, which can at times sound like a construction gang at work, or at least a major case of tinnitus, goes quiet. We've earned some peace.

Whitman suffered some hard days before he became the poet Walt Whitman. He had trouble getting work and holding on to it; he may have been prone to depression. But his struggles with the health of his mind were not as severe as those of Virginia Woolf, whom I consider perhaps the most heroic of writers.

On at least three occasions in her life, Woolf went completely mad. She succumbed to bouts of what was probably schizophrenia. She suffered from illusions and delusions; she heard voices. She believed that the people who loved her most—and she earned a great deal of love in her life—were her enemies and were out to destroy her. She had to be confined in her room and watched twenty-four hours a day. When her husband, Leonard, whom she clearly adored when she was sane, came into the room she was capable of screaming the vilest execrations at him. She hated herself and she hated the world.

Writing did not make Virginia Woolf sane. To be honest, the strains of writing might sometimes have pushed her into mental turbulence. But Woolf lived to write. Her productivity was spectacular: novels, short stories, brilliant book reviews, and polemical prose like *A Room of One's Own*. Beyond that there were her diaries: five thick volumes that contain some of her sharpest (and her funniest) prose. And letters. Woolf adored the act of writing. She threw herself into it like a warrior into the fight.

When she broke down, there was one goal that was preeminent in her heart: to get well so that she could write again. She fought against madness, hung in, suffered, and persevered, so she could get back to doing what gave her life fullness: writing.

Eventually Woolf succumbed. Her suicide note says that she could not put Leonard through another round of madness and she did not think that she could sustain it either. She dropped thick stones in her pocket and waded into the river.

But she lived long enough to write *To the Lighthouse* and *Mrs. Dalloway* and the essays that have brought hope to what are now generations of aspiring women writers. (And a few men too, dare I say?) Woolf fought to stay sane and fought to write. No athlete coming back from injury, no politician returning after defeat to try it one more time could possibly possess the guts that Woolf showed in her hunger to be sane and to write.

She and Papa Walt, two of the strangest and most idiosyncratic writers who ever lived, have a great deal to teach us about writing and the achievement of sanity. Honor them for their works, of course. But for their example, we should honor them, too.

TO SEE WHAT HAPPENS NEXT

WALTER BENJAMIN TELLS the story of an impoverished schoolmaster who lives far out in the countryside—which I'll elaborate just a touch. Every season the catalogues from the great publishing houses in Berlin and Munich arrive in the mail. He reads them through with avidity and with awe. Wonderful books, wonderful—there are so many he would like to read. His salary is miniscule, though. He can barely afford his rent. But these books—one way or another he must have them. The titles promise amazing thoughts, revelation perhaps. But he looks down at his frayed cuffs and wonders if his linen will hold out one term more.

So what does the schoolmaster do? He picks out a choice title or two from the catalogues. These are the books he would give anything to read. He writes the name of the first one down on a sheet of paper and then he sets to work. He sets to work writing the book for himself.

The story of the schoolmaster may sound like the tale of an eccentric—and a hyperbolical tale at that. But the more one thinks of it, the more one sees it is a tale of the writer proper.

Or at least it is the tale of many writers. They write because the books they most want to read are not available to them. They write because they are not really disposed to read exclusively what is on offer in the library. They write because they are curious. They want to know, somewhat as we saw Whitman did, what kinds of stories and essays and poems lie latent in their own minds and spirits. They write to find out what will happen next.

For truly, in writing one often does not know. Writers who make outlines and graph it all down to the most minor character's most negligible utterance tend to be assembly-line writers. They are often writers for money—not the worst identity in the world, but not the best either. They are like dictators for a state yet to come into being. They want to exert control over the whole production. And the production then feels overmanaged, overcontrolled. In genre writing this may be the idea. But the authentic writer wants to surprise her readers. More important than that maybe, she wants to surprise herself. This sort of surprise, as I've suggested in the last chapter, is one of the greatest pleasures in writing.

"I never know what I think until I hear what I say." True—often too true—for many of us. But the writer is someone who can be surprised and delighted by what comes unexpectedly forth when she sits down to write. We know more than we think we know; we feel more; we have observed more and even thought more. There is, we think during our good runs, something like a creative unconscious. While we've been going about our business, it's been gathering perceptions and organizing ideas and preparing fresh forays. When we get on a roll, that part—whatever it is, wherever it is—seems capable of endless invention. The birds wake early and they sing until noontime. Then maybe there is a bout of melody in the late afternoon or even under the approving silver face of the moon.

There is a part of us always eager to let us know what happens next, always ready to surprise us with the depth and heft of its perceptions. It is—dare I say it?—a source of (potentially) endless pleasure. Real novelists wake up in the morning and when it is rolling well they wake up and tell themselves a story. They are parent and child. They write the tale and enjoy the pleasure of its being told, too, for they do not really know what is going to happen next until it does. They never know what they think and feel and trust, until they hear what they say or see what it is they write. A writer is her own Scheherazade. She spins a tale for her own enjoyment that delights the world. Or it doesn't quite—but to her on those perfect mornings it was the best tale in town. It was better than reading Tolstoy, superior to immersing herself in Proust, and far in happy excess of the mutterings of the gossip down the road, in the phone line, or on Snapchat. Inside the writer lies the child who always wants to hear the tale the writer herself has to tell. The child does not know what is going to happen next—and neither does the writer.

But for this to go on—for the writer to find out what is best in him simply by sitting back and hearing what he says next—conditions must be met. There are often, as we've said here, rules to the game. There is frequently a price for the ticket. That which is most creative in the individual is a god, or at least a feisty little demiurge. Anyone who would write does well to learn the ways of his inner god, and to observe its favored forms of gratitude, sacrifice, and recognition.

I heard a story once about the poet Theodore Roethke that went this way. Roethke's work had not been going well. He had been drinking extensively. It is no secret that Roethke was given to drink. He often drank as a prelude to writing and then as a reward. There were apparently periods when he drank as a substitute for writing. But in the midst of an especially hard period, Roethke received a pure visitation. The poem unfolded itself from end to end; it came as if it were a piece of dictation. It came something like the way the lines of *Paradise Lost* came to Milton. The blind poet woke early and they seemed to appear out of nothing. When he had twenty or thirty lines in his head, he would call one of his daughters to take dictation. I need to be milked, he called out. From what I can tell, this is Milton's only recorded joke, unless you include the one about vegetarianism in the middle of the great poem. "No fear lest dinner cool," the poet says about a fresh-harvested vegetable feast. But that's about it.

Roethke's poem, my storyteller told me, struck him like thunder, lightning, and finally fresh spring rain. He wrote it all down and he felt cleansed and light and pure. Then what did you do, his friend asked. Oh, Roethke said. I did what I usually do when I get a poem like that. This was to fall down on his knees in the middle of his living room, burst into tears of joy and gratitude, and thank whatever power it was that had given him the gift.

Few writers go quite this far; Roethke seemed to have gone all out in many things. But I strongly believe it is important to say thank you. It makes sense to express gratitude to the force that is both you and more than you and that enables you to create stories and make sense and conjure a trope where before there had been nothing. Academic literary critics like to say that past writing begets writing. They think there is a template for a novel of a certain sort or a poem or an essay and that writers internalize those templates and then give them a twist or a tweak. (Bloom, more generous to creative souls, talks about the "swerve" away from past creators.) From this vantage, writers are plagiarists. They find much more than they make. But ask one of those critics to give you a passable sonnet. No dice! He's read a few thousand. Why didn't he manage to internalize the template? The empty page is just that—empty. And people fill it with the effusions of heart and soul. (Though often they'd better revise to make the effusions a bit less effusive.) And after they do so—after they've enjoyed the vast pleasure of creation—I think they are well advised to proffer some form of thank you.

The force that is inside the writer and that is him and not him—the force that makes it worthwhile to hear what you say—needs to be thanked, just as it needs to be coaxed into action in the morning with this ceremony or that. (Sharpen six pencils—not five, never, never four!) But I think the internal spirit of writing needs more tending to than that: a writer, like a lover, has to go beyond hellos and good-byes.

The writer Sven Birkerts says (in sum) that he may write for an hour or he may write for three—or he might write for a mousing fraction of sixty minutes. It doesn't really matter. All the rest of the day is dedicated to making that writing time possible. Maybe he needs some hard exertion—classes taught, walls mended, other peoples' essays whacked into shape. (Sven's an editor.) Or maybe the preparation is gentler—so-and-so many football games to be watched, hot baths taken, walks in the woods during which one does not walk terribly fast. Gabriel García Márquez had it right—and it is maybe *the* central piece of writer's advice. "A writer," says Gabo, "must know how to relax." But her relaxation is a different sort than the other woman or man's; her hammock swings for a purpose. The writer has got to learn how to make the force of writing available to himself—to hear what he says so he can know, for the time being, what it is he thinks.

But what precisely is this force that begets writing? Is it possible to define it? One might begin again with Freud, who did a lot to define the unconscious, though the definition is partial and thus rather misleading. If you invert much of what Freud said about the unconscious, you begin to get at the truth of the writer's creating force. Freud believed in the unconscious, of that there's no doubt. His first real book, *The Interpretation of Dreams*, affirms the centrality of an unknown region of the mind. It's unknown, yes, but it is also potent: it may even determine the course of our lives. The pressure of the unconscious is what causes us to dream. Then comes Freud's justly famous formulation: "A dream is a disguised fulfillment of a repressed wish."

Why repressed? Why isn't the unconscious available to the conscious mind? Because the wishes clapped down in the unconscious are forbidden wishes. They are murderous, sexually perverse, oedipally charged. We can't allow them into consciousness because they are too disturbing. If we were compelled in the middle of the day to entertain a fantasy about sex with mother, father, sister, or brother, we would be deeply disturbed, pushed to the brink of fear. At night, the dream censor—the bar between the unconscious and the conscious mind—becomes slightly more tolerant and the forbidden wishes make their way into our minds, albeit in disguised form. And that, naturally, is why dreams are so weird. They are always submitted to partial censorship.

Freud wanted to protect us from the unconscious, or at least from being influenced too much by it. Every now and then he slips and admits that something fresh can come out of sleep and dreaming. He remarks casually that often when he gives himself a problem—even a tough intellectual riddle—before bed, he wakes up and finds he's untangled the knot or (being Freud) that he's cut the rope with a stroke the way Alexander did with the Gordian knot. How did this happen? His unconscious did the work for him. But then he goes on to forget that he ever said as much or felt so. Mostly the unconscious is a danger; it leads us back over forbidden grounds. Its desires are the desires of childhood and it behooves us to have adult desires. Take your cues from the conscious mind, Freud says. Respect the unconscious, but don't be directed much less determined by it. Acquaint yourself with the creatures of the night, but don't let them drive the vehicle or even fill out the trip plan.

Freud affirmed again and again that the unconscious is regressive and fundamentally pathological. It is not creative. Thinking so, Freud suggests, was the error of generations of poets, and in particular the romantics. Coleridge, who did not interest Freud at all, but is the preeminent philosopher of Anglo-American romantic poets, strongly believed in the creative unconscious. For him, it was clearly linked to the imagination, which "dissolves, diffuses, and dissipates, in order to recreate." That sounds like Freud's dream work—except that for Coleridge the result can be magnificent poetry rather than disturbing dreams. The wonderful Coleridge poem "Kubla Khan" rose up from STC's unconscious as a dream—assisted of course by a bit of opium.

Writers tend to know that both Freud and Coleridge are right. There are toxic dreams; we all have them. And there are times when the unconscious, or whatever in there does the writing, grows ill. It produces only stale images, tells only stories it has told before, lets the judgment overmanage the product, turns writing into assembly-line work. There supervenes the horrid condition called writer's block, which is, truly, too unpleasant to talk about. Though when a student who is producing nothing, *nada*, and *rien* claims to be down with the malady I think of the wise words of a certain longtime writing instructor. They go something like this: You? Writer's block? No, sorry. Writer's block is for people who have *written* things, and usually pretty good things. And then for whatever reason, they can't write anymore. You don't have writer's block. You just aren't writing. A touch harsh, but there it is.

That's the downside—the debilitating side of the unconscious. But when the unconscious has been made healthy and strong—by whatever means you use to make it so—then one feels there really is something creative that is both oneself and other than oneself. Granted it has its own strange ways and often needs extensive care and feeding, sometimes with multiple naps included. But anyone who has worked away at writing has experienced those days when something else within is doing all the work. Before Saul Bellow started writing *Augie March*, he was in Paris on a Guggenheim Fellowship and he was genuinely blocked. He was on a novel about two men in adjoining beds in a hospital, and the streams were all clogged up at the source. (It's a premise that might even block Shakespeare, unless he thought to make a comedy of it.) Suddenly a new idea, a new voice came into his head. "I am an American, Chicago born—Chicago, that somber city—and go at things as I have taught myself, free-style, and will make the record in my own way: first to knock, first admitted; sometimes an innocent knock, sometimes a not so innocent." Well, you know the rest, or if you don't you have a treat coming when you crack that book.

The point is that by whatever work of quotidian magic, Bellow opened up and made contact with the source and let it have its way, he said of *Augie*. "The book just came to me," Bellow said. "All I had to do was be there with buckets to catch it." That doesn't mean writing isn't about rigor and training and all the rest. It doesn't mean hard work doesn't apply. But there does come a point for some writers when the work has been done, some discipline's been acquired, the desk's clear, and the unconscious is tipping, if ever so slightly, in Coleridge's direction rather than Freud's. Then it's time to play around a little, write freely, find out what the spirits have on their minds this morning—see what will happen next. It may be hard to get to that fine point, but when you do, what greater pleasure is there?

TO FIND YOUR MEDIUM

I N MY EXPERIENCE, if you've just met a writer and want to have a rich conversation with him, ask him how he writes. (Or ask about cats.) I don't mean the entry strategies (meditation and pencil sharpening and the rest). Those are too personal. You're trespassing on the writer's spiritual life when you try to pull that. I mean the implement question.

Do you use a pen? If so what kind? Is it a jazzy Montblanc or a Bic with the nether end chewed just so? A pencil. Well, OK. But a No. 2 or a 3? And what sort of paper? For a long time I was disposed to the yellow lined legal pad. Makes me feel official—lawyerly. But I'm also free to make plenty of mistakes. It's yellow, throwaway paper. I'm just practicing / this doesn't really count.

Does your dinner companion use a computer? Probably so. But when in the process does she, as it were, go electric? Does she write drafts on the machine? But then isn't it hard to redraft, given that it's all so well laid out and authoritative looking that it would seem a little sacrilegious to mess with it?

And if your new acquaintance uses a computer, what kind?

And what's the best of all possible programs for composing novels or screenplays or stage plays or epic poems or haikus, as the relevant case may be? If you really want to get on the writer's good side, and maybe learn something to boot, ask about the *history* of her writing technology. Yes, even the pencil is a form of technology, if you understand technology as McLuhan did. Technology is the extension of man, the sage of Toronto said. So a pencil might be said to extend the hand and likewise with a pen—and give the hand a capacity it doesn't possess, the marking capacity. And a computer—what does that extend or enhance? The whole human brain maybe (at least once the computer has been connected to the Internet), or at least a significant part of it.

Why does a writer use one implement rather than another? Why should you? Is it possible, vaguely possible, that you can improve your writing, or even get it going, simply by using the right tool? Picking your tool can be nearly as important as deciding whether it will be fiction or nonfiction, short stories or poems. Getting the medium right is one of the great pleasures of writing—but it's often a pleasure that needs to be renegotiated through the middle distance of a writing career. What worked early may not work quite so well as the road winds on and the clock goes around and around.

The writers I grew up admiring all seemed to have the same method. They wrote in longhand. They slaved away with pencil (or pen) and paper, sweating and steaming, as though they were humping crates in a factory. This writing was *work* dammit. They blotted their papers and crossed out and shed ink over them as though it were their heart's blood. Then they crushed the papers like tiny cannonballs and sent them flying across the room. At the end of the day, it looked like the room was full of tiny boulders stained blue with angry ink. But there was something left—a page or two that might be keepable. And then? And then?

Then they had it *typed up*. They gave it to their typist, who tended to be a girlfriend, a wife, or a secretary who had been with them for two decades. Early that evening, or maybe fresh the next morning, the writer has a clean, clean copy in hand, which he then proceeds to scourge with his pen, until rents open up in the skin that is the paper. Then it goes back to the typist again. Even if the writer types himself, he sends it off to the typist to retype, so it's clean as a freshly laundered Brooks Brothers shirt, which he will then, of course, submit to war-time trials.

What was up? Writing technology used to be a lot more primitive than it is now. Sure. Anyone entering the game could feel certain he was going to engage with a lifetime of Wite-Out and correction tape, as well as with machines that commonly threw off one letter from overuse, inevitably a vowel, almost inevitably one's favorite vowel. (If one may have a favorite vowel.) But to remedy this situation there was for the writer, or anyhow for the successful writer, the typist, who turned your volcanic flow into the cold, authoritative word.

That was a guy thing, to be sure. Males have almost never been confident in the writer's role, especially when what they wrote was fiction or poetry. They needed to make the game more masculine. Hemingway helped us out of course with the fishing and hunting (and the remarkable early prose). But maybe it wasn't enough. The business of passing on one's pages to an indentured typist—which still goes on, I can attest—was in part the business of trying to seem like a man of business with a secretary, or maybe a high-ranking personal assistant of some kind. But whatever rationale existed for the scribble and pass it off technique is now gone, usurped by the computer, which is not only an expansion of the writing hand, but a marvelous expansion of the human brain.

Writing on the computer gives you everything that possessing an amanuensis ever could have and more. It is magic, or about as close to magic as writing can get. Press a button and the letter appears; press a few more and you have a word. More still and sentences are inclined to appear. In not long a paragraph is what you have. How do you write so much someone purportedly asked Lytton Strachey. I write one word and then I write another, he sagely said. On the computer, writing that way is as easy as pie. Your shoulder doesn't hurt (usually), your back feels fine (you can half recline when you write), and if you take some precautions, your hands won't succumb to this syndrome or that. And—most magical of all—you can erase without effort and without defacing your paper in the least. You can edit with ease. Try this! Try that! See how it sounds. Keep a half a dozen drafts of the piece and then compare. The computer is quite simply a writer's genie. You call it by simply opening the screen of your laptop and then it goes magically to work for you. Your password is the only alakazam you need.

And it will correct your spelling. No small thing if you happen to be, say, me and could spend ten minutes trying to piece out a word like, oh, amanuensis. If you don't have a fact or quote at hand, turn to Lord Google and lo! The computer is a demigod—and it is completely at your disposal. It does your bidding over land and water like those angels in the Milton sonnet. The computer is a miracle.

But should you use it? The problem with writing on the computer—or rather *a* problem with writing on the computer—is that writing can quickly turn into typing and typing into writing. Truman Capote of course said something like that about Kerouac's *On the Road*, and it supposedly bothered Kerouac for the rest of his days. That's not writing; it's typing. The writer who uses a computer for the first draft is maybe creating an illusion for himself. It looks so finished. It looks so clean. It looks publishable. Darn it. It looks virtually *published*, and all after a first draft. The softness of the keys, their responsiveness to touch, the bright almost glamorous light that comes off your page—it's all so easy and so (why not say it?) beautiful. How can you not fall in love? How can you not tumble head over heels with what is nothing better than a first draft?

The form and the content, we might say, are at radical variance with each other. The form is slick, smooth, and lovable. The content on the other hand . . . Well, the content is the content of a first draft. The quality of the computer manuscript can sing you sweetly into feeling that your work is all done when it is anything but.

If you use a pencil and pad, or even a manual typewriter, your first draft will look like what a first draft most probably is: the dog's dinner. OK, no big deal. Time to fix it. But when your first draft looks almost like a sculpture in marble, why should you mess with it? Once you have something that looks that good it's hard not to let it stand as is. Oh, you'll go back through the manuscript and tinker of course: rearrange sentences, check facts, crush a few tiny, bug-like mistakes. But you won't be likely to do what many writers feel goes a long way to deepening a work. You won't start over with the raw first draft at your side. The cake looks to be already baked and iced. Add a cherry and a few sprinkles and you're done.

But for many writers what they want and need to say lies a few layers below the level of immediate articulation. Their first drafts come too much from that everyday self that does the laundry and takes the car in for servicing and goes to the movies to relax. For them, a first draft, even a promising one, stands there blocking their access to what genuinely matters. It's a barrier as much as anything. Hart Crane rewrote his poems so often that sometimes no really significant terms appear in the final draft that were present in the first. That's extreme. Still, for some writers the first draft, though welcome, is a little like Ahab's pasteboard mask. They have to smash through it to see what's on the other side. Tinkering is not smashing. Fixing the grammar will not blast them through the pasteboard to make contact with the real.

Do one draft, I tell my students. Then set it beside you and go into the second from the top down. I'm guessing that since the advent of the computer this advice has been observed largely in the breach. But it is the right idea, especially for the beginning writer. When Henry James—a master in his own fashion—entered his late phase he was able to dictate his novels. Joyce did much the same with *Finnegans Wake*. But one is not Henry James, and surely one is not Joyce, James, either.

Writing overall may have actually declined because of the computer: less consideration, less compression, more sheer text let loose on the world. They call it word processing. What's in a name? Word processing sounds like what they do in a word factory where volume and speed and efficiency overrule other values. Write your words. Don't process them. Computers are a pleasure, but a peril, too.

Posture is part of your medium as well. Hemingway wrote standing up. He brought himself to attention in front of his desk every morning and went at it. And what came out at least early on is what you might expect—clear, sharp, exact prose. He wrote prose that was *disciplined*. He stood at attention or something close to it, and he wrote prose that was also often at attention. He seemed to write the way a sentry on guard duty would, observing the scene with a cold, discerning eye. Not every writer's work lines up with his writing posture the way Hemingway's does—or the way I'm imagining it does.

But in writing, posture matters. It doesn't matter quite as much as your direct writing medium, maybe. But it is important what your body is doing while you do your work. For what it's worth, I tend to write first drafts half reclining on a couch. I want as much bodily ease as possible hoping that will translate into as much mental freedom as I can get. Body relaxed: mind and spirit relaxed and receptive. Or that's what I'm hoping for anyway. I think a lot of first-draft writing is associative; one idea leads to another and then to one more. What guides the associations? Who knows? I think if you've read a lot and thought some about writing, there are templates in there. You know what an academic argument feels like; you know how a short story can go; you have a feel when to glide into your ending if you're writing a poem. Those templates, I find, usually undergird your free, or almost free associations.

I, and probably most people who try to write, find a sense of ease and dreaminess more useful than what Hemingway seems to have wanted: discipline and distance. And I use posture to try to get that. Later on, doing a second draft, I'm more likely to sit up straight in a chair and focus. Sitting gives me a sense of schoolroom seriousness and I sometimes expect to see my old sixth grade teacher, Miss Smith, much beloved by me, though only in retrospect, looming over and judging what she sees. I'm glad I'm working on a computer; she won't have to see my spidery handwriting.

Dress can matter too, though it sounds strange to say so. A fine critic who teaches in New York could, it was said, only do his work—reviews for the *New York Review of Books* and such—after he'd showered and shaved close and put on a three-piece suit and adorned himself further with tie and cuff links. And he did possess a rather official-sounding voice—good for a critic no doubt. Though isn't writing supposed to be an alternative to a soul-chewing day job? I couldn't put on the tie and the links, unless it would buy me an essay like Eliot's "Tradition and the Individual Talent" (Eliot was perfectly capable of writing in a three-piece suit) or Trilling's on Keats (Trilling was wearing a jacket and tie even when he wasn't).

Most writers I know list in the other direction. One I've heard of teaches writing at a large state university. He's jammed his classes into a two-day intensive and when three thirty on Tuesday comes, he rolls into his house, climbs into his bathrobe, raises his hands over his head in caesarean triumph, and cries: "Weekend!" It's said that he writes all the rest of the week long and only really emerges from the robe when it is time to shower, sleep (nude, naturally, all emperors sleep in the primary), or fornicate. He needs to be relaxed and he is.

So check your wardrobe. If you write best as an emperor, then dress as one. Some no doubt are prone to athletes' togs—and if I'm right, the old line is true and athletes and writers have more than a little in common. And if you're hoping to be a cultural statesman, by all means look the part.

But more important is the transcribing medium. I'd think twice about falling first into the computer, especially if you're just starting out. Get a pencil; get a pen. Get your papyrus of choice and have a go at a first draft that goes from brain to arm to hand and then flows onto the paper like a magic spell. (Writing *is* magic when you think about it. Words that were in your mind come out and stand in place on the page and all can read—read, as it were—your mind.) Words are holy: direct connection with them is sublime.

TO SKIP WRITING THE GREAT
AMERICAN NOVEL

THERE ARE TIMES when I wish I had been alive in 1814. There is to be sure a good deal I would miss: I appreciate penicillin, advanced dentistry, and the power to hear any rock song I want (just about) anytime I want (nearly). But 1814 had its advantages, one of which was that it saw the publication of Jane Austen's *Mansfield Park*. However bad the food was then, however rotten the English weather, whatever the worries about Napoleon's resurgence and war with the French, one still had something. One had Jane Austen. At least the few people lucky enough or shrewd enough to read her did.

As everyone knows, all of Austen's novels are about the same subject: young women getting happily and advantageously married. Both words matter—happily *and* advantageously. Emma and Fanny and Elizabeth find the man who will fill their lives with joy, but they also manage to get, or in Emma's case to stay, rich. (The plot of *Persuasion* is a tad more complicated and *Sense and Sensibility* is not quite readable to me, though almost.) The plots are similar, but the characters are different, fascinatingly so; the dialogue is exquisite; and the texture—the lived experience of the young women and their suitors is rendered with such precise detail and such near to bursting intricacy as to make you ask aggressive and disagreeable questions. How could this person, this Jane Austen person, see so much of the life around her (and a few miles away from her) while the rest of us see so little?

For Austen's novels are contemporary, contemporary to her. She is looking out on her own social scene. She is writing about her times. The dresses her heroines wear are the dresses in the windows of the shops Jane Austen passed. (She could see those dresses in the milliners' windows; though she probably could not have afforded them herself.) The papers they read are the current papers; in Austen's provinces the London paper is a few days late and so it is for the newspaper readers in her books. At Austen's balls her dancers dance the right dances to music by the composers of the day; they eat what was served. They ride horses or coaches or walk (there's a lot of walking in Austen) as they would in the contemporary world at large. The soldiers wear red coats; the women wear muslin; the servants make their servile ways in homespun. The plantation Sir Thomas goes to visit in the Indies—leaving the young people to frolic (rather dangerously) at Mansfield Park—is the sort of plantation replete with slaves that a British nobleman might have owned in the early nineteenth century.

It's all there. Austen's world is Austen's world. She does what truly great novelists can do: takes her own time and metabolizes it into fiction. She turns the external into the internal. From reading newspapers and chattering with people and watching what passes before us, we gather a sense of the world we inhabit. But it is an external sense, a journalistic sense, a detached and small sense. We do not *know* what it feels like to live as we do, and we do not even know what it is like to know what we know. Thought and feeling, ideas and experience are unjoined.

Austen famously compared her work to minute carvings in ivory, and to this there is something. Her world is small. But she can make it feel quite central. If you've traveled with her and paid attention (Austen requires a great deal of attention), then you can know by association much about the life of her times. She hits the center of the bull's eye—though almost anywhere she aimed would become the center of the bull's eye, so much significance would she find there.

Great fiction writers offer many bounties, but one of them is to take their time and render it in words that let readers know what it is like to live—in their own moment. Don't we all know that? No. Absolutely no! Not in the least. We swim blindly through our days; we sleep even when we are awake. But there are some who *are* awake. They see what is before them and they have the added gift, combined with the discipline, to render it in words. Of these few Jane Austen was one. She wrote the great British novels—at least two of them, *Emma* and *Pride and Prejudice*—circa 1800.

The "circa" matters. No other form of writing is as time bound, time responsive, and time sensitive as novels are. The proclivity of the form, its grandeur and limitation, is encoded in its name: novel. It seeks to give you something new, something new about that which is new. Novels, good ones, turn the news into a form of secondary lived experience. They wrap up your time for you and hand it to you in a box of many pages. And as your time passes away, the power of the novel does, too. Novels are of their time. Lyric poetry may aspire to duration. Shakespeare made claims of longevity for his sonnets, but not his plays. And philosophers seek to speak truth to the ages. But a great novel is now.

It doesn't mean that a novel of the past can't be read with pleasure and profit in the present—far from it. But I think the power of fiction usually diminishes as time passes. The miracle is to take the present and find its significance—disclose its meanings—in the way no journalist or blogger or newsman or newswoman is in a position to do. The best time to read *Mansfield Park* would have been the day it was published. On that day its light would be strongest and most subtle and it would illuminate more areas of experience than at any other moment. Novels are news that are more than news. But they don't usually stay news forever.

Some are so strong as to shrug off the wear of time—or some of it anyway. We still want to read Proust and James and Woolf and Austen. But we would much rather read the Jane Austen of our times (if we had one) than the Jane Austen of her times. There is much that stays true over time and great novels can capture that truth, but we want the eternal matters joined with the immediate—and real novels do that.

That brings us to the great American novel—and your relation to it as a writer. I love the lines that are beneath the Statue of Liberty in New York Harbor, the lines about giving us your tired and poor, the huddled masses yearning to breathe free. And I love Woody Guthrie's "This Land Is Your Land" and think it should be the national anthem and be inscribed from place to place across the country. But I fear we Americans have another side and would find another fit motto if we dared. Americans: We want to have our cake and eat it too. Have you ever heard of the longing for the great African novel? The great novel of Asia? Nope. But the great American novel? You hear about that all the time.

Have our cake and eat it too: that's about what we want in almost anything and almost everything. We want to have complete domestic security all the time, but never infringe on anyone's civil liberties. We want complete national security all the time but never to mistreat a prisoner or to commit an aggressive military act. We want to spend all the money in our coffers and be certain that our kids will be able to pick up the tab when their turn comes. We want to have our cake and eat it too. We'll consume it with champagne and gusto. The having—the possessing—satisfies the good little citizen in us; the eating satisfies the spoiled little kid. Fun to be both—if you can manage to bring it off.

The dream of the great American novel is an instance of the cake-both-ways desire, albeit a fairly minor one. What we want is a novel that does two nearly incompatible things. First it takes its own moment and turns it, to use some shorthand, from journalism to art. The literary writer Northrop Frye tells us what happens. The historian tells us what happened. And the philosopher tells us (or presumes to tell us) what must happen. We want our fiction writers to tell us what happens now. They must let us know in sensuous and specific detail how it is with us here in the present. This is work enough. Years pass in which, one might argue, no novelist succeeds in doing this. At best, very fine novelists become contenders. They never get full agreement. There are those who believe that Jonathan Franzen rang the bell with *The Corrections*, those who believe that David Foster Wallace slammed down the hammer, sent the missile high, and maybe shattered the sound piece with *Infinite Jest*. But there will be no consensus. Philosophers talk about holding your time in thought. Fiction writers could talk—if it wouldn't spook them—about holding it in both feeling and thought nicely merged together. (You might call it, after Schiller, the merger of the spiritual and the material through play.) And that is a lot to achieve.

But the quest for the great American novel asks for more. Not only must the book summarize now, but it must also last for all time. It's got to capture the moment and every moment to come; it needs to be literature (what happens now) and philosophy (what must happen) simultaneously. This is virtually impossible. We want to have our temporal cake and our eternal (never spoiled) gateau on top of it.

There are novels that defy this difficulty. Joyce's *Ulysses* may be the most local, specific, time bound, historically evocative novel ever written, being as it is about one day in the life of Leopold Bloom, Stephen Dedalus, and Dublin, Ireland, the third protagonist of the book. Ah, maybe there is a fourth hero, the day in question, June 16, 1904. There is no more brilliant study of the way we are now—at least if you were alive in Dublin on what ought by now to be a holy day of obligation for all lovers of literature.

Joyce is of his time, emphatically. But the book's technique, or rather techniques, reach out ahead of June 16, 1904. *Ulysses* is written in every literary mode known to humanity and a few that are still not quite understood. You get overt narration (some), collage (in the wandering rocks), stream of consciousness (Bloom much of the time), drama (Nighttown), catechism (a chapter of seemingly endless Q&A), and in Molly's chapter, the last of the book, what's surely the grandest novelistic monologue both heard and overheard (Bloom's are overheard) of all time. Every fresh form of writing in *Ulysses* reveals new possibilities for literary technique that we can still learn from. But they also explore the workings of consciousness (in *Finnegans Wake* Joyce will explore the unconscious, though an unconscious much unlike Freud's). Expand the resources of consciousness; blaze some trails for the development and the fulfillment of the mental powers. I think Joyce does that, too.

So OK, OK, one instance: not the great American novel, but surely the grand Irish novel. And maybe, maybe there is someone out there who can complete the American task. (Maybe *Moby-Dick*—but maybe that was more a book of the future than of its 1850s present, and as such a stunning anomaly.) But it's a high mountain to rope your way up and even Joyce (shh, don't say a word about this to anyone) can sometimes be in his attempt to merge the eternal and the temporal with all the literary razzmatazz what one can only call—well, you know, oring—with a *b* up front. Put it this way: when we go to Nighttown, I reach for my pillow. And Joyce's decision to yoke his book to Homer—which I'll bet came late in the composition—makes things more mannered and dry than they need to be. Eliot lapped this stuff up in his essay on Joyce and the mythic method—but then Eliot was using Joyce to try to teach us to read his favorite author, T. S. Eliot. Jane Austen, on the other hand, is entertaining and instructive every moment of the way in *Emma* and *Pride and Prejudice* and *Mansfield Park*. She's great, a wonder. I only wish I were alive in 1814, to read her as she truly deserves to be read.

So don't be bothered by the beckoning of the great American novel, or the beckoning of greatness, period. Remember that sloppy, inviting immortal beginning of Bellow's *Augie March*. "I am an American, Chicago born—Chicago, that somber city—and go at things as I have taught myself, free-style, and will make the record in my own way."

Freestyle. That's right. The novel's a mess and probably won't outlast its time by much. But freestyle: that's how you do it. Free. And what pleasure is greater than the pleasure of freedom?

TO FIND BEAUTY AND TRUTH

W HO CAN DO justice to the subject of writing and beauty and truth in a few pages, a few books, even a few lifetimes? Surely not I. Others with greater powers and larger claims to achievement (by far) have dropped their buckets into this well and often what they've come up with has been impressive, though not yet (as I see it) definitive. One thinks of Horace and Longinus. One thinks of Blake and Shelley and Hazlitt. One thinks of T. S. Eliot and of Virginia Woolf. This is stern company and one does not seek entrance to it readily.

But one might say to start that writing's ultimate goal should be to do something for others as well as for oneself. Writing is about enlarging the mind, the expansion of consciousness, the addition, as the critic R. P. Blackmur liked to say, to the stock of available reality. We're told that writing is about finding the truth and infusing it with some beauty, too. But what does that mean?

The philosopher—the pure philosopher, the follower of Plato—seeks ultimate truth, Truth with a capital *t*, if you like. He aspires (it usually is a he) to capture truths that will be true in all cultures, at all times, in all places. If Plato's depiction of the three parts of the human soul—the rational, the spirited, and the appetitive—does not hold as bindingly true for Americans in the twenty-first century as for Athenians in the fifth, then Plato fails.

It's impossible you say. We know now that truth is contingent on history and culture—and on race and class and gender to boot. Maybe, maybe that is so. But why then do we still read Plato? Why do young people all over the world still open his book and find there not a subtle indication of ancient attitudes, but instead a vision that thrills them with its aptness—its candor, its shrewdness, its (why not say it?) claim to truth? Plato is a contender for the ultimate palm. Of this I at least have no doubt.

But while Plato can be poetic, he is not quite a poet. That is to say that his truth is not always beautiful. The Myth of Er and the story of the ladder of love that Socrates imports from Diotima in *Symposium* have their glamor and allure, certainly. But there can be—there often is—a slight brittleness to Plato. He smacks too much of the logician. There's a whiff of the schoolroom. Above the door of his academy, it's said, there was a sign posted: ONLY THOSE WHO KNOW GEOMETRY SHOULD ENTER HERE. Is all truth geometric, or based on geometry? Some, no doubt. But there may be more—and that more, that other kind of writer's truth—may be what inspired Plato to banish the poets from his Utopia.

What do we mean when, in Keats's spirit, we want to fuse truth and beauty? Or—in Horace's version—we hope to inter-mingle instruction with delight?

What the romantic poets offer is a version of truth that is personal. This is how I see it. This is how it is and was for me. (And here too is how I hope it may be for you!)

What some writers do, the romantics among them, is to let us know what is true for them. The question of how it is becomes how it is for me. Do they risk self-indulgence? Solipsism? Sure—and worse: this way madness can lie. But who knows that perhaps Plato was wrong about universal truth and the best we can hope for is to see the world as it truly is *for us*. Perhaps there are only individual truths—and by affirming our own we open up the possibility for others to go on similar quests. My exploration of my own mind widens the area of the possible for the minds of others Mailer tells us (and rather apologetically tells himself). Who knows? Stranger things have been true.

The writer who seeks personal truth almost always seeks something along with it. He seeks something that might be called a writer's beauty. By that I mean he not only wants to unfold his vision—his truth—but to convey the *feelings* that are part of seeing the world as he does. He is not detached but immersed, not authoritative but questing, not godly but human, as the sage says, all too human.

Literary beauty is distinct, it seems to me, from the beauty of a water lily or of Monet's rendering of one. It does not offer the possibility of detached contemplation that Kant commends. It doesn't offer alluring purposiveness without any purpose and lift us above the push and toss of the world as it is. Rather literary beauty may give us the feel of the belief it infuses. The work sees the world a certain way—all right. But what is it like to see the world in that way? How does it feel? Tolstoy and Virginia Woolf differ not only in subject, emphasis, and scope, but they differ also in the music they make and the music that makes their visions what they are. Tolstoy is stern and strong and somehow both passionate and detached. (This happened. This will pass.) Woolf is alert, immersed, present, and very nearly participates in the dramas she unfolds. She lives and joys with Mrs. Ramsay. She dies with Septimus Smith.

She does it (and he does it) through something it is not quite right to call style, though style may be the best word we have for the phenomenon. What I mean is the braiding of the sound and the sense of a piece of writing, so the way the author sees and the way the author feels about what she sees become united. Frost says that style signifies the way the author took himself in relation to what he has to render. Did he believe it fully? Partially? Did it fill him with joy? Loathing? Some impossible but possible combination of the two? Style is too external a word for this power of fusion. You put on the right pants or pantsuit and you have a sartorial style. But I think the beauty of writing—the fusion of sense and sound—doesn't involve put-ons of any sort. Rather it involves what one might call an integration of character.

Truth and beauty (even if it's the author's particular truth, the author's beauty) fused together suggest a mind that knows itself as far as minds can do. The mind of this kind of writer not only knows what it sees and understands, but it also renders what it feels like to see the world in such a manner. When Woolf writes a description of Mrs. Ramsay, we feel not only her powers of perception of a character but also the spirit of admiration and sorrow and exasperation and love, mostly love for this figure. It's there in the prose—in its music and in its metaphors—though it is not easy to isolate it and break it down into elements.

An imperfect illustration: look at the movies. All movies are scored. Music plays virtually all the time through virtually every film. And generally, alas, one *hears* the music. At best it is mildly agreeable. At worst it is an intrusion; it feels too overt, manipulative. I don't need to be *told* how I should feel. Just make me feel that way, if you can. But sometimes matters are different. Sometimes the images and dialogue on the one hand and the score on the other manage to fuse. You don't really hear the music; you don't know it's going on. It's part of a unified piece.

The analogy doesn't fully work because a movie score is still much more extraneous to a film than literary beauty is to writing. The expressive beauty of writing—the melding of sound and sense—is what nonutilitarian writing is all about. It's what lifts a piece of writing up from being just adequate to being something special and memorable. Few works of verbal art that do not possess it in some measure have a chance of surviving.

But this all sounds rather high-flown. What could it possibly have to do with anyone who is just starting out as a writer? Or even someone who is in the middle distance of the race?

Most people, I think, feel that sense comes first. We figure out the plot, the argument, the central metaphor, then on we go. This is no doubt true sometimes. But I think there's another truth that's often allied to composition—one less commonly understood. That is that sound can create sense. What I mean is that when we start writing, what we're looking for is the right voice: the right degree of irony, the right level of sobriety or exuberance. And then tone leads to text.

I'm inclined to work quite a while until I have a first sentence I like. (Or in a longer piece, a first paragraph.) And by "like" I mean like the sound of it: that sings, that jumps, that rocks, and maybe rolls. Or at least it doesn't pancake down on its face. And once the voice—what I think of as the literary beauty—is there, then the words usually come. The voice is the key that opens the door to sense. Music makes the movie happen, not the reverse.

This may be why a lot of writers listen to music while they write. They want to purloin a rhythm, grab a sound. I'd rather find my music myself, but on this, each to her own.

Yet this is worth underlining. In writing, beauty can bring on truth; sound can be the creator of sense. Why this is is hard to say. Do we have different voices living in our spirits? Do we possess—and are we possessed by—different selves? Where do they come from and what are they? They surely don't have a place in Plato's map of the mind or Freud's or St. Augustine's.

I've never dowsed for springwater and despite temptations (I live on the site of an old farmhouse) I've never taken a metal detector to the grounds around my house. But writing is sometimes a little like dowsing and prospecting. We search for the right voice, the right tone, the right rhythm. Then, led by the music, the ideas come pouring in. Or they stay in abeyance because we approached a piece in the wrong key. It's not that our ideas were bad per se. We couldn't get to the good ones because we did not find the song of the inner oracle that spoke to the matter at hand.

For a long time, I wrote books and essays that were—give or take—literary theory. My wife, a fiction writer to the tips of her fingers, couldn't really give a toss about literary theory. But I always showed her the opening paragraphs of anything I might do on Derrida or Foucault or their compeers. She'd read it, maybe not quite know what was being said, but with great confidence be able to say: "You're on!" And also, from time to time: "You're not!" This had nothing to do with the content—only with the music, or lack thereof. "Not custom or lecture, not even the best," Whitman says, "only the lull I like, the hum of your valved voice." When you hear that hum, some truth may be on the way.

I think one of the reasons we care about literary writing and prefer it by far to what we can get in the newspaper or the review is this attempt to fuse feeling and thought. The reviewer and the newspaperman want to get the feeling out of the way. They often want to sound universal, authoritative, imperially anonymous. The literary writer lets us know how it feels as well as how it is, and in a unified and intelligent way.

In a famous essay, T. S. Eliot told us that fusion of thought and feeling had passed away from literature sometime around the English Renaissance. He called it "the dissociation of sensibility." Before that point, Eliot says, writers commonly thought and felt at the same time. His crucial example is John Donne (the essay is on the "Metaphysical Poets") who conceives a blush and conveys the experience of it at the same time.

Eliot claims to be cross with the modern world for doing away with the possibility for this sort of cohesion. But I'm not at all sure he's right. The idea is a part of his overall polemic against the current world. But the truth may be that for most of us the unity of thought and feeling may have been broken. We are pragmatists in our public lives, romantics in our private. But putting it together—that is no easy matter. In fact, it never was and never will be. It seems to me, for what it's worth, that Eliot (among many others) does so again and again. He had the mind of a metaphysician (his thesis was on F. H. Bradley) and the heart of a religious quester. Poems like "Little Gidding" do a fine job of recomposing that dissociated sensibility. For it is a state that bothers us all and has, I suspect, from the start of rationalized and overrationalized civilization.

Writing that takes as its ultimate goal the integration of feeling and thought can create fine results, and on two levels. It can provide us with work that truly lives, the kind Keats says we could prove upon our pulses. And it also brings us together into something like unified being. When we laugh we know why; when we weep we do, too. Feeling never goes far from intellection, intellection from feeling. We are, insofar as a human being can be, united within ourselves.

THE WRITER'S WISDOM

TO MINE A FRESH EXPERIENCE

I SOMETIMES LIKE TO think that writers age backward, a little the way Merlin was supposed to do in the Arthurian legends. Up to a certain point, they get younger over time—at least if you attach a certain meaning to the word "younger."

Quite simply, you get better at what you do as time passes. Writers often don't peak until they get into their forties and fifties. And if Yeats, who exploded creatively in old age, isn't exactly representative, he clearly shows us what can be done by an old writer—even when he takes that apparently most depressing of periods, old age, as his subject. Yeats sometimes loved being old; he had always pined to be wise and now he has some claims to be. He has seen much and he has thought it over. And words—Yeats is never at a loss for glorious words. When he says that this everyday world is "no country for old men," he takes us to a new land, Byzantium, that's richer yet in imaginative possibility.

It's here that the analogy between the writer and the athlete falls apart. The beginning writer and the athlete just starting out have much in common: they're both acquiring their craft, learning their moves. By the time the athlete reaches her peak, the writer will probably be nothing more than an advanced beginner, still stuttering, still stammering, still not sounding like herself. But days go by. The big-time passer hurts his arm; the running back pulls up lame; the lineman's knees wobble. But the writer surges forward, getting stronger as she enters her thirties and forties, getting her game on when the athlete is relegated to the announcer's booth or the brown card table where he sits signing the memorabilia. Writers do fade, but they enjoy long-stemmed growth, often into old age and some-times to the end. Old age is harvest time for the writer, and if he has written and read with integrity, the harvest will be rich in yellows and crimsons and gold.

Old age provides subjects for the writer. There is the world around her as seen from the vantage of long experience. There is also the life of the aged man or woman as it is day to day. People have never lived as long as they do now. They have never counted as many years. This gives all of us aged and aging writers access to fresh experience—the experience of being older than people (or at least people outside the pages of the Hebrew Bible) have been before.

Writing in old age, or late in life, has another advantage, too. What people commonly say about aging and memory seems to have some truth in it. We elders may not know where we put the car keys, our car keys, but we can wake up remembering the cars our mothers and fathers drove, and what it felt like to lie supine in the backseat, on the way to get ice cream, or to visit a relative in a parlor or a cemetery. Though the present has faded to a lighter shade, the past opens up. It's as though we've stepped inside one of the photographs that was left in sober black-and-white silence in the picture album. And then, suddenly, suddenly, all is color—the way it was for Dorothy when she whirled out of Kansas and came down in the kingdom of Oz. Suddenly, we are children again—children who see with both childish eyes and the eyes of experience, too.

Everyone who is disposed should try, when she reaches the season of ripened memory, to write a book about her past. If the gone world truly opens up for us as the present world recedes a bit (those keys, those keys), why not acquiesce and be students and connoisseurs of our own early days? Who knows what discoveries we will make?

For the writer who has been at work a long time and has mastered some part of his craft, old age can also be a blossoming time. He's made the right moves. He's begun to begin. He's slammed through the wall that separates writers from nonwriters. (Even if he had to, well, do something as bizarre as making like Hunter S. Thompson to do it.) He's got his set of rituals and incantations to get flying above the walls of prohibition and commonplace mind, or to let him slide elegantly below. And he's learned all the things writers need to know, or at least that he as a writer needs to know: he's got the right device (and it's probably not a computer, or not exclusively one); he's comfortable being alone; he's jazzed at the thought of knowing what he thinks by hearing what he says, not scared; he's aware that sometimes it's the music that matters most when you start to write and so he listens, or asks someone he loves to listen, for his proper melody. In other words, he's learned all this book has to teach and probably a lot more.

Then he can sit down, get into gear, start writing, and see that the face reflected in the words on the page is his own, and no one else's. He is his words and his words are him, even when—and maybe mostly when—they surprise him the most.

That happens in old age, if it happens at all, and even then it probably does not last. But when he writes and he sounds like himself and no one else, and does so without trying all that hard—well then, something very good has happened. The writer has made it home to himself.

TO BEAT THE CLOCK (A LITTLE)

I'M AN OLD writer, and really it's not too bad. Being most
other things when you get old is less than wonderful from
what I can see. Old movie star, old athlete, old CEO, old
construction worker: usually not so good. Old writer: so far not
half bad.

They talk about laying money aside for your later years. I've
tried to do some of that, yet I haven't done nearly what I should
have. Though I plan never to retire from my job teaching at the
University of Virginia, factors larger than our own desires can
intervene. There's sickness; there's growing so far out of touch
with students that you can't really understand them, nor they
you; there's the possible insane desire of one of my younger
colleagues to possess my large-windowed office, which might
result in who knows what. But barring those events, or my
ability to negotiate them (that younger colleague who wants to
bask in my sunlight better know what he's getting into), I
intend to stay with my job. And just as important, I intend
to stay with writing. Because writing is something you can do
when you're old—and if you could do it passably when you

were younger, you can probably do it at least semi-passably during the gold (or gold-plated) years. Surely in time the workings of the mind will slow and slide to the point where even you can't make much out of what you've put down on the page, but that may not be for a very long while.

So I'm not saving much money for retirement—and what's left in the account when I go I hope that my sons (both artists) will get. But I consider writing to be a sort of socking away of pennies for the purposes of the future. By writing I'm investing in at least a partially livable old age.

Now I'm not talking about the prospect of a late-career blast, like the one Henry James had when he dictated those three astonishing semi-readable late novels. I'm not even talking about a run at the bestseller lists like the ones Bellow and Roth managed in late or latish innings.

I mean writing as a consolation, vocation, and pastime for late life. I'm also talking about it as a form of mental health sustenance, especially well suited to the old. The mind's a muscle. (This much has been a premise of the book.) And though I haven't a single scientific study to back me up, I'll advance the hypothesis that writing can help keep the mind sound in old age. Physical infirmity is one sorrow; we've all had a taste of it before we've been old. The back goes out; the leg twists and the next day we're lurching forward on crutches; the dentist looks inside our mouths, doesn't like what he sees, and does three hours' work, only to release us with the promise that we'll be back in three days for another round. We've all had a taste of the physical infirmities, an amuse-bouche as they like to say, even if we've been pretty lucky.

But of the sliding mental powers we know little. We've lost our keys many times, even if we're twenty (especially perhaps if we're twenty), but we know what the damned things are. They're keys, for goodness sake. (Babies love keys: they open the portal to adult life, or adult life under capitalism. Keys matter.) To forget your husband's name, to not know your four-year-old grandson when he races down the driveway to show you a new gizmo you have every right not to know about, to be unable to address an envelope, to be confused every point of the waking day: this is harsh punishment.

I'm not sure. No one in a lab coat is behind me on this. But I'm betting the exertions of writing can cancel some of the mental sorrows of old age, or at least postpone them for a while. If you do not use it, you lose it. And to write well (write and revise and laugh at it and improve it) you've got to use it. There is no other way. The cliché doesn't lie. (One of the joys of getting old is that you can use clichés with almost full conviction and near abandon.) You *make* sense. You make sense through writing and you make sense through talk—good talk. But there isn't always someone around who can hit the conversational ball back over the net with the right velocity and challenging spin. So writing is the best default. It only requires you, a pencil, and a sheet of paper. (What inventions they are: paper and pencil. I sometimes look at them both, pencils in particular, and smile with strange gratitude.) Writing helps you learn to make sense. And when you do that and you get good at it, or as good as your lights allow, you may keep doing it long after the investment banker and the real estate mogul and the doctor who told you that you had better live better than you do are slipping into the twilight. Maybe. I'm not a scientist and I don't know. But Socrates (greatest conversationalist on record, maybe) was sharp enough at seventy to talk rings around the citizens of Athens, and Sophocles was still writing topflight plays into his eighties. The playwright competitions held in Athens in Sophocles's extreme old age? He won one at about the age of eighty-seven.

But maybe the best thing about writing in old age is that you can write as yourself. This sounds a bit strange and isn't easy to explain, but here goes. Old age (of which I'm a fairly youthful exemplar) is as Schopenhauer and others have told us the time of self-acceptance. We've become who we are going to be and that's pretty much that. The writer in old age doesn't need to get up on stilts. He's tried that before. He's tried to write what the superego demands. (The death of most academic writers.) Or he's tried to write in the voice of the superego. (That's the death of his reader.) In old age, he is no longer aspiring upward. He can write as himself.

Himself? Who might that be? The most optimistic lines I know of about identity in old age come from Confucius. It goes this way: at fifteen I set my heart on learning; at thirty I stood firm; at forty I had no more doubts; at fifty I knew the will of heaven; at sixty my ear was obedient; at seventy I could follow my heart's desire, without overstepping the boundaries of what was right.

Confucius is Confucius—one of the sages of all time. But the point for all of us is that in old age he became himself. He no longer had to strive and strain. His deeds and his sayings as they came at the moment and off the cuff were his own and they were, all things taken into account, quite good.

What the old writer writes, when his faculties are still intact, is himself. He's not pushing it too hard. He's not trying to grab the fruit at the top of the tree, which may not be ripe at all—or if ripe, not terribly tasty. He's happy with what falls into his lap. He doesn't revise all that much, except to correct the technical mistakes his fading eyesight makes inevitable. (More on this in the next chapter.) Keats was surely thinking about writing as a young poet when he made his famous observation about the way poetry ought to come into being: "If Poetry comes not as naturally as the Leaves to a tree it had better not come at all." But such easy coming for poetry is a sign of self-acceptance— something the old writer is more likely to possess than the young. He's already had his shot at matching Tolstoy, if that's what he's wanted to do. Didn't work out, in all probability. (Though I persist in thinking that some of the best of current novels have probably never seen the light of print.) And now whatever blooms on the trees of his imagination, he finds himself grateful for, grateful and glad.

Shuffleboard, whist, bridge, hollering at editorials in the *New York Times*—all these pursuits have a couple things in common. All are penchants of the reasonably upscale elderly; all are dismal. Doing the crossword puzzle is no joy either I'll bet. But if you can write, you can engage in something that is dignified, serious, potentially humorous, and maybe even noble. Looking back and writing about what one knows, or believes one knows, putting one's life into words—this is dignified activity. This is worth your time. Does writing keep you young? Now there were only two real young writers that one can think of offhand—that is writers who have written with *genius* from the position of extreme youth—Keats and Rimbaud. But the rich detachment and absorption that writing demands are qualities of deep and thoughtful middle age. Thus this chapter's slogan. Writing: it keeps you middle-aged.

And perhaps giving the green light to oneself in old age might help one hit one's stride. It's possible that one of the best goals for a writer is to become *identical* to his work. That means he's the same person in life that he is in his writing. He talks like his books—which speak modestly and generously and sometimes even wisely. (The young Susan Sontag expected her idol, Thomas Mann, to talk like a brilliant book. Instead, she said, he talked like a book review.) And when you meet him on the street or the subway he's got some of that good stuff to give you, too. Holden Caulfield talks about wanting to call up the authors of the books he likes and ask them a few questions and make friends. And how many young readers have wanted to call up Salinger and have an intimate chat after finishing *The Catcher in the Rye*? I surely did. But Holden figures that the authors probably put the best of themselves into their books and he'd be disappointed. Maybe he's right. Probably so. At least for the young writers: the man or woman you encounter in their books is a self-projection into a desirable future, a persona. But the old-man writer? Imagine encountering Montaigne. The great old essayist called every spade a spade, and every tool a tool, and talked of the most exalted things in the most available words. He was someone who could talk of simple things in simple and memorable terms and complex things in the simplest and most illuminating terms possible. I'll wager that Montaigne talked the way his books did, even if J. D. Salinger never could have. Montaigne's essays constitute a prolonged memoir; and we might say that a prerequisite for such writing is the self-acceptance that old age can bring.

That would be something—talking like your books and getting away with it. It would take time to achieve that status; you'd need to accept yourself, sure. But the self in question would have to be well worth the acceptance. It'd have to pass muster, survive judgment. The young person becomes himself when he leaves professional school and takes the first job or opens a business or buys his mother's farm. The writer may not fully become himself until old age: the moment when he and his books become one. And that is something worth working (and waiting) for.

Another way to describe the self-acceptance and wholeness that writing in old age can bring is to say that in old age one can sometimes all but stop revising. (It's a scandal, but I believe it.) More of that next.

TO STOP REVISING

R EVISION IS THE god of many writers and the god of all writing programs. And I admit that I have been—and in some measure still am—a congregant in the faith. Revision builds better writing. Revision can not only build character in itself, but it can also provide a template for how character overall is built. (Try it again. And again. And again.) People who achieve a lot usually start with some ability, and then over time develop a tolerance for failure that's not unlike a champ boxer's tolerance for getting hit. (A tolerance for failure is different from an attraction to failure, or an addiction to failure; those proclivities are far from uncommon and tough to kick.) Revision is all about failing, acknowledging the failure, and hitting it again (and again). The devoted revisionist knows that nothing is ever quite right and nothing is ever quite finished. You never really finish anything, Truman Capote said. At a certain point they come and take it away. (Capote was lucky to have a "they" who wanted to take it away and then pay him for it, but that's another story.) Revision is about goat-like toughness, and character and fortitude. It draws on and enhances almost all of the cardinal virtues. Who then can speak a word against revision? Who then, especially having spoken more than a few words on revision's behalf, can gainsay this noble process?

Well, why not? Here we go.

One of the virtues of writing in old age, I'll dare to suggest, is that one can dispense with a good deal of revision. Self-acceptance and experience, the virtues of the old writer, can sometimes make revision superfluous. It is what it is—because we are what we are.

To teach writing, one understands, is to teach revision. Join a writer's circle or an MFA program or an online school that gets you corresponding with a writer (for a fee), and the emphasis will be on writing and then rewriting. Your teacher will boast about how she redrafted a story ten times, or a poem fifty. Your fellow students will be seen slug stepping out of the coffee shop, looking like they're just over the flu. But no flu—it's simply that, as they'll proudly announce, they just completed another draft. Are they done? You ask them with full solici-tude. In some writing environments, being "done" is the equivalent of siphoning money from departmental petty cash, then spending it all on a lavish lunch. No one is ever done: they simply come and take it away from you. And if no one comes—which is likely—then are you ever done? Tomorrow the coffee shop sloucher will be at it again: revising, revising, and revising.

Isn't there something a tad Puritanical about it all? Isn't there something a bit masochistic going on when you take revision to the point where you become a member of the holy church of revisionism? You can leave it to Americans to take an activity as potentially joyous as writing and turn it into a soul-slamming job. We don't feel good unless we believe we're earning what we get, earning in triplicate. There's too little belief out there in the god of writing, the god who simply drops one in your lap from time to time, the way the god did for Roethke. And for no other reason than that she feels like it.

When that drop occurs (if it does), have the character not to sit down and start revising wholesale. Because in writing there is such a thing as grace, such a thing as blind good fortune. You get the right subject, and the right genre, and the right weather (I like fall and spring) on the right day. Maybe you're in love and maybe you're just out of love. Maybe you fasted and prayed and maybe you ate and drank and made as merry as your belly and heart would allow. But now you have it, and this time, aside from adjusting some spelling and checking a fact or two (Bucephalus or Bellerophon: which is which, really?), you're golden. There are times when vision does not require revision; ask the visionary saints and they'll tell you.

And sometimes the best thing to do with a piece that isn't working is not to bring it into the factory of revision, turn on the assembly line, get on your goggles, bring out your welding tool, and start sweating. No, sometimes the best thing to do when you've laid a bad egg is simply to walk away from the nest. Get gone. Throw the darned thing out and start something new. You can advance by leaping from endeavor to endeavor, as well as by trying to repair the broken-down model that's on blocks in the driveway. As Ralph Waldo Emerson, the sage of Concord, tells us: "Power ceases in the instant of repose; it resides in the moment of transition from a past to a new state, in the shooting of the gulf, in the darting to an aim . . . The soul becomes."

War wasn't the right theme for you; iambic pentameter isn't your music; you sound too much like T. S. Eliot for this to be yours. So run away. Be like that follower of Jesus in the Gospels who is with the Savior in Gethsemane. When a Roman soldier grabs him by the cloak, aiming to arrest him probably, the young man takes off. He slips his way out of his cloak and runs naked into the dark. So try it. Run naked into the dark and soon you may see some light.

We all know about the Indians' ceremony, much observed all through these states, of potlatch. At a certain point every year the tribe got together and burned everything its members did not need and many items they thought they did. They burned lodges and they burned clothing and they burned saddles and they burned their weapons. They wanted a new start and they knew that you cannot make a new start in old circumstances.

If the tribes could nobly burn their all, then surely some of us can afford to burn a manuscript, especially one that has been giving us nothing but misery. Print it up, take it outside, light a fire, and feed the flames. And by the fire's light it'll be very surprising if you don't conceive of something new, or at least hear a fertile whisper or two around your ear from the crackle of the flames.

When the fires were over, the Indians had a great feast (I commend this part passionately) then set to making their lives again, better than before. The computer has many advantages, but it's not as easy as it should be to jettison a textual weight once and for all and *start again*. The text simply looks too good—too clean, too polished, too publishable. In fact it looks to be almost already published. Still, sometimes one must cut it loose.

People stay in rotten marriages; they maintain rotten jobs; they live in crap neighborhoods. And sometimes this is out of grim grinding necessity. But no one needs to make the killing interest payments on a so-so piece of work that will never get really much better than it is. Declare bankruptcy in the court of yourself; tell the judge to cram it and hit the street.

I think the current love of revision has much to do with that grand MFA and now undergrad institution, the writing workshop. There's much to be said for the MFA in fiction, not least that it gives writers a home, some bread and milk and maybe a little wine, and keeps them from having to work ten hours per in the bowels of the dry cleaner's. (Whenever I enter a dry cleaner's and look in the back and hear the thrum and smell the chemicals and feel the steam, I say a prayer of thanksgiving.) But the MFA has its downside, too.

There must be something called workshops. To these workshops you bring your story or poem, as if it were a busted-up automobile, and the senior mechanic and the mechanics in training surround your ride and while you obey an enforced silence tell you what must be done to repair it. (Truly, you are not allowed to talk as they analyze your vehicle. This is something I could abide for ten seconds or until the first truly flat-brained comment, whichever came first.) Then you go off and commence repairs. Occasionally I'm sure your colleagues will tell you, though not in so many words, to take your vehicle to Moe's Scrap and Salvage. But mostly it's all about repairs, which is to say revisions.

No religion of revision, no MFA programs: I think that's pretty much the truth. No MFA programs, nowhere for experienced writers to go and make decent coin and no place for young writers to hole up and work. I'm all for the hideout for the kids and the decent coin for gramps. But at a certain point, our cover stories risk becoming our stories and we get serious about our deceptions.

There's much to be said on the side of revision. And earlier in this book I hope I've said some of it. But there are limits to the religion of *once more unto the breach*, and for all writers—beginners and pros—they are worth keeping in mind.

But so far in doubting revision, I've employed what the sage calls "a poor external way of speaking." There's something truer and maybe more profound to be said about putting the revision religion aside in the late game.

Isn't there a sense in which all revision is lying? That's putting it hyperbolically, but maybe revealingly, too. Shouldn't the writer be able to present himself as he is, rather than as he can make himself appear to be after endless sand-and-buff sessions? Whitman says—and he's said it plenty in this book—that "This is no book. Who touches this, touches a man." He means himself of course, and it was true for that first volume. It simply poured forth: life and all it means (here in these states) according to "Walt Whitman, an American" as he calls himself partway through the poem. There is no author's name on the title page of the 1855 edition of *Leaves of Grass*, just a picture of Walt in open shirt and slouch hat, "one of the roughs," as he likes to call himself.

In certain forms of writing, I want the writer coming at me direct and unprocessed. Reading some overedited books is like listening to studio jazz albums—too highly produced, too short, too unwilling to let the tattered flag of the self fly. (Whitman calls the grass "the flag of my disposition, out of hopeful green stuff woven.") I like writers who show you the holes in their elbows and knees, and who ramble and even rant a little sometimes. I like Montaigne in his essays and Emerson in his journals and strange spontaneous-seeming books like Ann Marlowe's *How to Stop Time*. Critics are accused of breaking butterflies on the wheel. Too many writers break their own butterflies. They try to hit the street with a factory shine. They smell too much of new-car interior, for me. Whitman of course liked to talk about a part of himself he called the "real Me": the part that stands both in and out of the game, "compassionating, idle, unitary." And he gives us that part and its perceptions as immediately and crudely and sweetly as he can. Later on Whitman went to work trying to write Walt Whitman poems and he seems to have revised them until they could all be dropped into glass bottles full of formalde-hyde. Against revision? I'm at least against the sheen that comes from the *appearance* of too much revision and that appearance is everywhere. Turn a page or two in the *New Yorker* if you don't believe me.

But there's something deeper at stake here. I think the evolu-tion of a writer into his final phase can be an evolution beyond revision. That is to say he has become identical with his voice and writing sensibility. He doesn't have to strain; he doesn't have to struggle. What comes out when he sits down on a pretty good writing day is his and that's that. Tinker as he will, it won't get much better and maybe it will get worse.

All his life, he's been trying to find a way of speaking and writing that fits with his sense of the world. For a while that involved a lot of tinkering and messing and fooling around. He had to stand on tiptoe to sound the way he wanted to; he had to find a soapbox and get up high. But late in the game he can echo both Popeye and Ralph Ellison's Invisible Man (and a larger creative force that doesn't need to be named): I am what I am. This is the moment of quiet and assured self-acceptance, the moment when striving stops, the self is unified, and no longer lives as much in becoming as it does in simply being.

The palm at the end of the mind, as Wallace Stevens calls it, has been reached, and there is nowhere further to go—which is both a sorrow and a blessing. You've done your work; you've figured it out. You've become yourself, as Nietzsche liked to say. But you're also the old man or woman sitting on the dump. "One sits and beats an old tin can, lard pail. One beats and beats for that which one believes." Everything you say and write is your own, and yourself and you are at home in your mind— and that's a fine thing. But the next change is the last one.

TO REMEMBER

FAULKNER FAMOUSLY SAID that "memory believes before knowing remembers." Though no one is terribly certain what he meant. What Faulkner *may* mean is that there is a deeply sunk layer of memories we are connected to and committed to, and that exist on a level beyond conscious knowledge. We don't *know* the past; we feel it in our bones and blood, and we live it out day to day. (Especially, no doubt, if we live in the South.) We all have pasts, both personal and collective, and writing is one of the best ways to recover them. Whether what we recover bears much direct resemblance to any kind of objective truth (assuming one exists)—well that, as Faulkner suggests, is an open question. On a level too deep for ready questioning, memory is disposed to believe.

Is there a value in remembering the past, putting it in some kind of order, maybe turning the events of our lives into a story— or maybe finding the story that is latent in those events? I think there is and especially so for the writer in old age. Is there a genre more fitting to late life than the memoir? The material is all there before you. You probably have the time. Why not let it rip?

There are obstacles, of course. And perhaps they are more intense for the old writer than for the young. Will anyone care about my book? That is a way of asking: Will anyone care about my life? Will anyone, does anyone, care about me? The ultimate form of getting someone else to care, according to many, is getting one's book published. And the fear of failing at publication may be at the root of failing to write the book of one's life. I'd like to zap that fear away, for the young, but for the old in particular. Writing is not about publication, though publication *can* be a splendid event. Writing is about writing. Some of the richest writing is about the life and times of the writer. And unless you are a superb and rather long-winded talker, with an audience of patient, loving listeners, then writing is the only way to set out the story of your life.

I applaud the memoir genre. I like it that individuals sit down and try, usually in something like the way Aristotle commends, to see their lives as having a beginning and a middle and at least a provisional end (the end supplied by the moment of composition). Many of the narratives handed down to us through culture and history don't really work anymore. Many people can't attach their lives to a religiously based story about salvation, or a patriotically based story about their place in the drama of the nation. They may take some sense of identity from their families, but it doesn't prove to be enough to give them what all of us, I believe, crave: a sense that our lives have meant something and continue to.

We want to believe that our lives have a shape and that they add up to more than what our bank accounts and tax returns and school degrees testify. We want to feel that we progressed toward a goal or goals. We tussled with this dragon or that; we overcame obstacles; we pulled matters into place.

And then, from a resting spot, however temporary, we can pause and look down at the progress of our lives and feel a sense of unity and order. What better time to do this than in old age?

Some literary critics will tell you such order is always imposed, and that it has been fabricated and falsified. Really all there is to any life is a string of chance events. We don't make our own histories; history makes us, or race does, or biology, or social class. But more than likely it's all a matter of chance, a spin of the wheel. And we don't know what's going on. We never see the wheel; most of us don't even know we're in a casino.

But I see it differently. Those qualities of plot that Aristotle valued so much have been around for a long time. Stories that matter have protagonists: The protagonist has a task or tasks to do. He enters into combat, enters into strife. He finds he doesn't know what he thought he did about the world or himself. But then in the long run, he emerges, knowing more than when he started and feeling the pleasures and the sorrows of his experience. There's no way to prove it, but it seems to me that conventional ideas about plot reveal important truths about life. We do struggle and strive, we do exert our wills, we do desire to make ourselves better women and men. But *how* we wish to do this—through getting money or status or getting very high and staying that way—can often be flawed.

The premise of what we call the life story or the memoir is that we are creatures who seek to learn. We want to educate ourselves in the ways of life and we believe that we often do. We screw up, granted. We make messes and then compound them. But humans are united (just about) in their wish to learn from the messes they have made and to improve. We all want to attend the school that is the world, and in deciding if we pass or fail its manifold tests, we finally want recourse to only one schoolmaster, and that is ourselves.

Poetry, John Stuart Mill said, is not heard but overheard. And memoirs, the genre of our moment I think, are usually overheard: it is not a man speaking to men, but a guy talking to himself that makes a memoir. The reader of the memoir is often a bit of an eavesdropper, and not every conversation one hears from beneath the eaves is an edifying one. I often find that certain memoirs don't matter enormously to *me*. I have different dragons to fight and the author can't make his bestiary into anything close to a universal one. But I love the *idea* of memoirs.

Everyone should write one, or everyone who has even a tinge of an appetite for it should. Anybody who is drawn to writing and is in search of a subject could probably not find a better one than himself or herself. Writing personally teaches many virtues—among them, how to take oneself. You can't sound like a monarch, but you can't sound like a clown either. You've got to develop a degree of irony about yourself that fits the narrative you're unfolding. How much skepticism is due your younger self with her dreams and plans? Or maybe it's the older self more prone to concession that needs to be treated with a slightly harsher tone than the young aspirant. You have to figure out your life, or a significant portion of it. You have to look back and see who really mattered to you and how. You have to see what incidents shaped your trajectory. In short, you have to brood on what you've become and how. You need to take a few steps toward knowing yourself. And then—well, you have a pretty good base for figuring out what you might try to do for the rest of your life. Or maybe you see that the past has been all about fate and chance anyhow and you relapse into a kind of opiated ease in regard to future plans. Don't bother chasing your destiny the Bedouin saying goes; your destiny is always in pursuit of you.

One of the best things about memoirs is that they are not autobiographies. Most autobiographies are written in stone—chipped away with care and precision, concerned about how posterity will feel and what the neighbors will think. They are self-justifying, posturing affairs that usually read as though they have been translated (badly) from the Latin. An autobiography is an attempt to deliver your own eulogy—in fact, to be completely in charge of all your last rites. It's a posthumous piece of writing. Memoirs come from the middle of the journey. Or often better still they come from the later phase—and they don't set out to get the writer elected to high office. The people who write the best ones *try* to be honest. Oh, they may fudge this or that detail and swell a story beyond its verifiable bounds. But emotionally, they try to get it right. Emotionally, they are usually willing to let it rip.

Hey, the memoirist says, this is how it feels to be alive. It hurts! It's grand, awful, amazing. But mostly: It hurts! Pleasure comes and goes. Pain is a guest that checks in and stays around—and sometimes monopolizes every room in the house. Autobiographers are topflight politicians and scientists and Nobel Prize winners (and near-miss runners-up who're still pissed). They are always looking for significance—their significance in particular. Memoirists are Frankie and Mary and Joe and Kashi and Mohammed and LeDonna; they are groping around the way real humans do for some meaning. It's a noble quest, or at least an admirable one, even when it doesn't go all that splendidly line to line.

When people finish their memoirs they rush to the publisher's office, or they try to. Most publishers throw heavy bars across their doors. Everyone wants to publish his book and if he can't, he feels himself a failure. Not true! Bad idea! Are musicians not musicians because they never cop a record deal? Is there something ignoble about the jam session and, as Joni says, "Playing real good for free"? Not a bit. People should be able to write and feel proud without ever being published. Writing is a human right (the pun tells us so) and humans should be able to do it without being judged as failures for not making the professional cut.

In that sweet rock song, Joni looks at the one-man band by the quick lunch joint and she envies him. She says that she plays for fortune and what she calls (with nice irony) "those velvet curtain calls." But the guy on the street sending sweet sounds out of his clarinet is a free man; he plays what he wants. And he doesn't play for cash or to inflate his ego. He gives his music to the world as a gift and he makes it for himself, for the pleasure of it. "Nobody stopped to hear him," Joni says, "though he played so sweet and high." Well, OK, but he made the music and no one was telling him that he had to cut a little off the end and squelch the solo and mute the controversial stuff about death row in Texas or AIDS. No one was listening? Not really. Another real artist—Joni—was. And she was missing the days when she could do what the street corner guy could: play real good, for free.

Not writing your memoir because you won't get it published is like not playing ball in the gym because you won't be going to the NBA. The game is still there; the game is still the game.

Why not jump in and have some fun. People think getting a book published is everything. Then they get a book published. And so they think this publication ride was a bumpy one. My editor got fired midproject, my agent got into crack, my publicist got a divorce. Next ride will be better, so they work hard and think only of the glorious day when the book will come into the world. Books aren't babies. For the mother (and father too I hope), the birth is everything. For the writer the gestation is the wonderful part. The putting of the words down on the page and then fussing with them and fussing some more. If you like that sort of thing, there is nothing like it. Asked about what his life as a writer was like, Tobias Wolff reportedly answered: Boring unless you happen to be me. But if you are me (the implication goes)—not half bad, even rather amazing.

There are primary rights in this world that aren't specifically mentioned in the Constitution. You have the right to pray and to make music and to make love without being graded on a skill scale of one to ten. You are also fully licensed to write under exactly the same standard. (Or so say I.)

Writing strengthens memory. One of the most enjoyable aspects of writing a memoir (I confess to three of them, with another in embryo) is the way the mind opens its doors for you if you'll stand outside patiently and offer an occasional soft knock. Screaming "open sesame!" probably won't do it. You have to show up every day with your bowl in your hand and wait. But lo, in time, one door swings open and a corridor appears—the past being as it is a mansion of many apartments. And down the aisle you walk.

Some of what they say about old age and memory appears to me to be true. One suddenly has access to the early years. I can now recall the snowsuit I wore when I went out to play when I was four. (I was wearing it when I pancaked down on my face and could not get up.) I recall the shape of the driveway at 68 Main Street and I can see that policeman walking reluctantly up to tell me that my dog, with the unremitting seal bark, has got to go. These recollections have not been available to me for fifty years and more. Now at sixty, here they are. But don't ask me, please, where I put the title deed to the old Volvo two weeks ago.

Life can feel thin day to day. We do our duty, we complete our errands, we repeat our repetitions. We feel sometimes as though we spend all our time skating on surfaces and that we do not truly live. (As the poet Matthew Dickman says, "I made my plans. / I never arrived. I ate my food. I drank my wine.") People use journals to solve this difficulty. They make every day a word-worthy occasion. They delve keenly into what is before them and they find the meaning they can in buying baby formula, shopping for groceries, reading a snatch of a story, catching an installment of *Game of Thrones* on TV. Here in everyday life the journal writer gets at what Wallace Stevens called "the plain sense of things."

The memoirist adds density to his life through recollection. The repetition compulsion that is daily life gives way to a complexly layered sense of being. Freud compared the psyche to the ancient city of Rome, in which building was built upon building: there's the Forum and the Palatine Hill, under which the ruins of a mud-hut village are there to be detected by the close observer. So it is with the self. The person we are sits atop different phases of identity, different layers of being: all of them shape each other and the first layer is shaped by the simple contours of the land from which it rises. To begin to excavate those layers is to begin to touch the mysteries of living in the world and to make our lives as miraculous to us as they deserve to be. The memoirist restores wonder to the day to day through the patient and supplicant art that is memory. For the old writer there are more layers, more revelation, more gold.

The mind strengthens itself though writing. The more we use our memory the stronger the muscle becomes. We think better than we did, for in certain ways thought is memory and memory is thought. When the seminar was puzzled by a line of Wallace Stevens or Hart Crane (so difficult he must at times have been a puzzle to himself), a teacher of mine asked us a question: "What instance in literature or in life does this remind you of?" That question, simple as it is, always had the virtue of getting the group unstuck and moving. Memory creates analogies that enable us to see what is in front of us. Yes, I've been here before give or take and (give or take) I know what to do.

Frost said, with a certain measure of exasperation, that he could do with a bit more praise from critics. They needed to understand that writing could involve feats that ought to fill them with admiration. They should see, said Frost, what a feat it was to be reminded of this by that, what a feat it was to think of the perfect metaphor at exactly the right time. And it *is* a feat too, to be thinking about climbing a birch tree all the way to the top, being careful not to lean forward too hard and send the slender birch groundward before you reach the top and to be reminded of filling a glass with liquid to the very top and then (you know what this looks like) over the top, but without spilling a bit. The metaphor—and what is metaphor but being reminded of one thing by another?—occurs in "Birches" and it is, genuinely, a feat of memory and imagination.

Thought relies on memory; if you cannot remember you cannot think in any but the most rudimentary way. Writing brings memory to bear and enhances its powers. Writing is the great school of the mind, from the writer's Day One to old age and to the end of her life: there is no better one.

TO GET BETTER AS YOU GET OLDER

"THAT IS NO country for old men." That's William Butler Yeats looking back at the world of nature, appetite, and generation as he sails away from it. He loved that world. Yeats was a vitalist and a romantic and thought for a while that his best inspirations came from erotic love, even when (and maybe especially when) that love failed consummation. He seems to have proposed to the woman he thought to be his soul mate, Maud Gonne, at least three times, and when she said no for the third, he proposed to her sister. (Their last name is pronounced Gun. Yeats should probably have taken heed.) Still, Yeats loved being in love and thought that some of his best work came from the flowering that takes place when one is smitten with a beloved.

In "Sailing to Byzantium," the poem with the line about the country that's not for old men, Yeats is both rhapsodic and exasperated about "the young in one another's arms" that he sees all around him. They call up comparison to "the salmon-falls" and "the mackerel-crowded seas": those lovers are vital, passionate, but they are not quite human either. They've become animals, though glorious animals to be sure. Anyway,

Yeats is no longer one of them. (At least for the space of this poem.) He's banished, or self-banished from their world. I find myself chanting the opening lines of "Sailing to Byzantium" to myself on the opening days of classes in the fall. The weather's warm, the young are in one another's arms (more or less) on the steps of Old Cabell Hall, the breeze is blowing. Everyone is eighteen or nineteen or twenty. The kids are wearing not too much. They're lying back—some smoking, some vaping. They are laughing even when their lips are set. This is no country for old men, or for old women, either.

That's true *overall*, of course. It's true in America; it's true in most of the West. This is not a country for old men. Youth is everything and everything that matters is young. We cherish the new, the novel, the latest, the fresh. We avoid what is fading and faded.

People peak early in our culture. The paradigmatic career is the pro athlete's or the pop star's. They flash like comets across the sky, flare madly, burn bright, and then slide downward losing light as they go, until finally they douse themselves in the brine. A few hang on, embarrassing themselves and us with their sagging bellies and plastic reconstructed smiles. They are there to remind us what happens to all things bright and beautiful and new. The former-jock-now-commentator lassoed into his uncomfortable tie, the old rocker in kicky new boots recall to us the glories of youth and the sorrows of age. Getting old is something that one ought to apologize for.

And often the old do. Oh, not in so many words, but they slink and scrape and bend and try their best to admire the latest and praise the new. They're sorry for having lived so long; they feel they're in the way. If only the young would indulge them a bit, let them live on with their remaining teeth and pleasures, gratitude would abound. This is no country for old men, or for old women, either. This is the country of the gleaming, chirping, tweeting, twerking new.

But to this rule, there is one exception. Not always, but most of the time it is true. Writers, real writers, often get better as they age. And even if their work declines a little, they can stay strong, keep producing, and keep doing what they love. They aren't like dust-binned CEOs or sidearm pitchers who have or haven't had Tommy Johns, or wrinkled race-car drivers, or admen whose careers have been added up by their superiors and found to be a few digits short. No: writers stay in the game until nearly the end, and it is not uncommon for their work to get better as time passes. Writers come in as tyros—skinny batters, easy to fool. Their gloves are bigger than they are. But while others decline from about their thirtieth birthday, the writer keeps growing stronger. He leaves the game more potent than he went in. Put it in physical terms—because, remember, the mind is a muscle. The writer starts with a stripling's physique. She works and works. She labors on and on. And in early old age, though her physical body may be declining, the body of her imagination is muscular and lithe. She's gotten better, often a lot, as she's gotten older.

"That is no country for old men," Yeats says. And he turns away from "whatever is begotten, born, and dies" and heads out—he's in a sailing ship, the sailing ship of his imagination—for something else. Which is what? What is the alternative to the life of the burbling new that surrounds him (and every writer in or nearing old age)? Before the opening stanza is over, Yeats offers some outright defiance to the culture of the new: "Caught in that sensual music," he says, "all neglect monuments of unageing intellect."

Sensual music—the music of desire is a form of enchantment to Yeats. It casts a spell upon the dancers and it is a lovely spell and it is lovely music, but the music is so strong that one cannot stop dancing. Try it and see. When you're young, you are always in thrall to desire. You perpetually want something. Most likely it is love (and sex). But all desires may in time become modeled on the desire for love and sex. All desires become similarly fierce, similarly fervid. You want and want and want and when you tire of wanting, you find that the sensual music is not only beautiful but also enslaving. You cannot stop desiring and acting, sometimes foolishly, on that desire. You cannot stop dancing.

Sensual music—it's so potent that you can dance to it throughout your whole life. When you are very young, you'll dance wildly. You'll be giddy, inspired, but also sometimes out of control. And when you're old, you'll keep dancing, especially if, as it is in the West now, the music plays as loudly as it does and is as alluring and well orchestrated as it is. You'll keep dancing even though you're out of step and you can hardly move your feet and you know you look silly and you are humiliating both yourself and the spirit of old age. But you cannot stop dancing. (I want an iPhone, I need a computer, give me some cash, I want, I want.)

A poet I greatly admire, Jack Gilbert, wrote a volume of poems in old age called *The Dance Most of All*. And Gilbert's evocation of the dance would be well understood by Yeats. I'm not going to give it up, Gilbert all but says. Even when I'm old I'm going to keep dancing, keep falling in love, keep being struck with awe, keep moving to the sensual music. He's going to be like old, old Tiresias in *The Bacchae*, who when Lord Bacchus comes to town gets out and grabs the thyrsus, sacred to

Dionysus, and shuffles his feet to the tambourines and gongs and bells. Gilbert and the ancient seer go in full well knowing what they are getting into. All honor to them. They'll go out as they came in, to the beat and the melody—to sensual music. But for the old man, and the old writer in particular, there are other possibilities: "Caught in that sensual music all neglect, *monuments of unageing intellect.*"

Unaging intellect. There are forms in this world that pass away and there are some, a few, that actually last. Yeats wants to leave the sphere of passing things and to dwell if he can in the eternal. He wants to give up on love and love's music and see if he can find truths that will abide. Are there such truths? Plato told us there are and Yeats could often believe there were, too. In Byzantium, Yeats hopes to make contact with art that will last and maybe to create some, too.

There may not be eternal art; there may or may not be eternal truth. But Yeats feels that though he's lost some valuable pursuits to old age, other possibilities have opened up for him. He's not stuck in time and the concerns of the moment, so maybe he's in a position to create something that will outlast him and will outlast time. He's optimistic, in other words, about writing in old age.

Most people see old age as sheer loss. Yeats admits that age is loss, but he affirms that there's plenty of gain to be had, too. For the first time in your life, you're pulled away from desire, and that hurts. It's humiliating to be old. You feel the grief of missed pleasures. But old age is also a time when, freed from desire, you can create writings you could not create before.

You need to prepare for this moment. You almost certainly need to do some writing when you are young and make the way ready. But if you've developed a discipline, if you've learned to read and think as a writer, if you've stayed with it despite the vagaries of publication and reviewers and editors and the people in your family and out of it who think you are wasting your time, then old age need not be a time of grief and sorrow. You're at least partially freed from that "raging madman" that Plato's Sophocles says held him in bondage through the first portion of life: his desires. And you have time to consort with longer-lasting matters. You have, in other words, something new to write about.

And that is exactly what Yeats—among the greatest of artists in old age—did. In his late seventies and early eighties, Yeats wrote his best poems. In them, he wrestled with what old age took away and what it opened up; he developed new perspectives on politics and culture and money and class and tradition, and of course on love. He felt he was seeing the world afresh. He did not repudiate his past adherence to love, not entirely. He sailed to Byzantium and embraced the monuments of unaging intellect. But sometimes he wished himself away from that place, too. One of his last poems has him foreswearing politics and worldly affairs and pining to collapse in the arms of a beautiful girl who is (ostensibly) much too young for him.

Old age is rich for the writer. It has its singular subjects and it has its particular freedoms. The aged writer can get better as he gets older not only because he knows more and has seen more, but also because a new state of being, the state of being potentially beyond desire, opens up and beckons him. And from that state he can see and feel much that is new and surprising.

Our culture is pitched to youth, and this is almost inevitable. But the old writer has much to tell the young about a life lived beyond the bounds of wanting. He can show them a world that is free from obsessive chasing and grasping, from getting and spending. And he can offer them the chance to take a breath, calm down, and to live there for a while.

Yeats knows what an old man looks like from the vantage of the young. "An aged man is but a paltry thing," he says. He's but "a tattered coat upon a stick." Surely it feels that way sometimes; surely the girl passing you on the street, fresh from the dress shop, can look at you and see nothing at all. One can become invisible. An old man is "but a paltry thing," a "tattered coat upon a stick"—no face, no body.

But not all the time, no. The old man who is a writer lives not only in the world of what is begotten, born, and dies, but in another world, too. And given the chance, he'll let you hear about it. For sometimes a soul can "clap its hands and sing and louder sing." Then the new world, which is the eternal world (maybe), opens up and we live beyond time. Seeing the world with full detachment, but not without humanity: this it seems to me is what a certain sort of wisdom entails. The country of wisdom: that is a country for old men and old women—and also for the young, whom we invite, most humbly and cordially, to join us there from time to time.

TO DRAW A CONSTELLATION

To the ancient Romans there were three ways of living on in the world once your physical life had ended. The first was the most obvious and immediate. You could attain immortality by doing great deeds. Caesar's conquest of Gaul and his ascension to absolute power in Rome were such deeds. And as Plutarch tells us, Roman history is riddled with spectacular achievements. Or you could speak words that would last forever. Cicero did that and so in his way did Tacitus. The last way to live for all time, at least as the Romans saw it, was to have children. They could carry your name down through the ages. To the Romans this was the least noble way to keep living after death. But it was also the most tenable and the most reliable, too.

Most of us will not write or speak words that will live forever. In old age we come to see this, if we have not seen it already. Our books and essays, our poems and plays will not find the eternal. With every passing century more splendid writing gets winnowed away from what is read from the past. We want to read what was written last week, or at the most last year, and there may be good reasons for this. But that means less time for the old books. No matter how good what we write today might be, it will almost surely sink into "the dark backward and abysm of time," to quote Shakespeare—that writer whose works almost surely never will so long as humans (or technologically enhanced or atomically mutated beings that resemble them) traverse the crust of the planet.

But our writings—great or small, published or locked down in the hard drive—can still serve us when we consider ultimate things. Our writings are our spiritual children we might say— offspring of the spirit—no matter if they be (as biological children sometimes are) stunted and strange in this way or that, or perfect only to ourselves and that not for as long as we would wish, for parental narcissism has its ways of being shattered. No, our writings carve our tombstones; they are our elegies. Or, maybe a better analogy (and surely a more optimistic one): our writings create constellations. They are the way we look back (or look up) and see that we have had a life.

A first book, as the writer Michael Pollan says, is a dot shining (however brightly or not) out there in space. But when you write a second book (or string out another essay, or compose a consequential poem), something happens. You have established the basis for a line. A segment connects one point to the next, and now everything is different. There is that which is above the line and that which is below. There is the slant of the line and there is the distance between the two points—a distance composed of how far the points are from each other and how direct the movement is from one to the other.

Now you have a writer's identity. Now you have a sort of biography. A dot is a dot. But a line—or a segment—suggests a being over time. This is where I started. This is where I went. Now, where do I go from here?

Suddenly, you are writing your life story. All at once, you are composing a biography. You are charting the course of your mind and spirit over time. No one is likely to sit down after I am gone and make the connection between my second book (on literary theory—hard-core academic) and my third, on the Gothic (written con brio with lots of reference to the here and now and only a little to the then). But *I* can make that connection. For me, it was about branching out—a move into a kind of language and thinking I hoped would be interesting to profs and nonprofs, to the clerisy and the laity, to use Coleridge's trope. I wanted to handle the now; I wanted to bring literary history to bear on the present, visual as well as literary. *Nightmare on Main Street* is a book about movies as well as a book about books. I wanted to spread my wings, such as they were, and look down on spooky Gotham.

But I think I'm right to believe that writing over a lifetime creates something of an intellectual/spiritual biography. You start one place, with your first published work or at least the first work of yours that gives you pleasure and satisfaction. Then you begin to move. You go from point to point, dot to dot. And partway through, your points—which may glow with starlight, if only to you—begin to form a *constellation*, though a constellation of a private sort, most probably.

But you're not done yet. There are more stars to place, a larger outline you still might draw.

Some writers put their stars so close together that no significant shape can emerge. And some put them so far apart that it's almost impossible to see from one to the other. The first writers tend to be very cautious: they're poets, sometimes, who have scored a hit with one volume and then want to do it again and again. The second type, the ones who want to expand so far into the void that their last effort is left eons behind, are sometimes the pros, the writers for money.

That some writers write the same novel (story, poem, play) over and over again is no secret. If it worked once, it may work again and it probably will. These are the cautious ones, the ones who are tied to a simple vision of themselves and what they can do. It's usually a matter of confidence. They never imagined they could have success of any kind. They were most unsure of themselves. They worked hard and they worked hard and then—voilà: there came something well worth saving and maybe worth showing to the world. And all were pleased and some were well pleased. So what to do from here? Repeat, reiterate: say it again. If Elmore Leonard ever wrote more than the one novel a hundred times over, I have not seen much evidence. Though sometimes the guys wear fedoras and sometimes they wear cowboy hats. (I love Elmore Leonard. I truly do—but still.) Something similar goes for my kindly and generous near neighbor, John Grisham. If you like one, you'll like them all because as Shakespeare's characters like to say, "All is one." If you write the same work over and over again and it succeeds, your spiritual autobiography is likely to be written in bank statements. Or as Bellow's protagonist says of a certain greedy-got character: she's writing her memoirs without a typewriter: she's using an adding machine.

Then there are writers whose books are so much unlike each other as to defy belief: one on insects, one on chamber music, one on the career of General Sherman. (I exaggerate, but you get the idea.) This is the career of a hobbyist who is ever acquiring a new hobby and dropping the old. His autobiographical dots can hardly be seen one from the other. They are points on a map that leads nowhere. The books may be good;

they may be not so good. (I bet on the latter.) But they don't really add up to a story about who the author was and why it might matter to him and to the people who know and (authors do inspire some of this; I'm sure they do) love them.

Some people keep track of their lives with their photographs and their home movies—and that's fine. But that's a record of the outer life, not the inner. They know themselves as others saw them, or as they would have liked to be seen. They've got a stack of laminated idealizations, or computer files of CIA length to click and slide through. But there's more to life than the way it looks. There is also how it feels. There's also what you did and how you changed.

Michael Pollan, whose idea of the dot-to-dot progress I've borrowed, started out writing about nature in general and gardens in particular. From there he went to architecture, studying the subject from Vitruvius to the present and building his own writer's studio to boot. Then he went to the erotic lives of plants—and the part that humans play (and are tricked into playing) in those lives. Then he moved on to food. What do we eat? Why is it as bad as it is? How can we make it a little better? This project involved the purchasing of a cow, which the author followed on its journey from the feedlot to you-know-where.

What holds Pollan's work together? Many factors: good prose, a hunger to make contact with readers, modesty, humor, curiosity. But what also holds it together is an unfolding interest in the places where nature and culture intersect: the garden, the dinner table, the roof overhead that shelters the man or woman the way trees once did and maybe will have to again. Pollan is interested in the subtle balance between nature and culture and particularly in getting that balance close to right. It's not right now—and that feeling is what tends to draw Pollan to a subject.

(Our diets stink. We live in goofy dwellings.) But Pollan is an optimist, and some of the pleasure of his books comes from believing that the interplay between nature and culture can be adjusted to make us happier and sustain what's best in the world of nature. We can get it right.

Did Pollan know that was what he was going to spend his life doing when, around the age of thirty, he wrote his first consequential article for a magazine, a piece on (of all things) compost? No, he didn't. I can say that with some authority because I was there. Earlier we collaborated on a very non-Pollanian piece about *Time* magazine. We called it "De-mythtifying Time." The *Columbia Journalism Review* published it, almost. There was no grand program on Michael's part, no game plan. He just followed his interests and his nose—talked and listened to people and figured out by a kind of ESP where his interests and the interests of many others overlapped. They too wanted to improve their lives in the immediate world. They too weren't willing to go Thoreau's route and climb almost all the way back into the heart of nature. They wanted a compromise, a dialectic.

Pollan has been arguing with Thoreau ever since he was an undergrad: a longtime love-hate relationship. Part of using your writing to understand your past life is seeing who—truly—your influences were and why they mattered to you. Major influences are like family: they are your spiritual mothers and fathers and just as precious sometimes in that if your parents gave you life, your writing teachers gave you motive for living. If that's too high-flown, you can at least say they gave you something to do. Part of what the writer looking at the endgame can do is construct her or his family tree: the influences, negative and positive and in between. That's another way of telling yourself who you are and who you have been. It's a matter of expressing gratitude—even to the ones that brought you to life through antagonism: negative inspirations. It's a matter of modesty. Though one might like to say with Milton's Satan that one is self-begotten and self-raised by one's own quickening power, it's not true (it wasn't of Satan either) and in the long run it's much less interesting than giving a full genealogy. The real writer doesn't have to hire a genealogist; he's already created his own ancestors. It's only fair and fitting that late in the game the writer draw the map and give credit where it's due.

And me? I recall one day a colleague telling me apropos of nothing much that my work was "all over the place." And that, of course, was more than distressing. There seemed to be something to it, at least on the surface. I had written a book on Freud and literature, one on literary theory, then that wing spreader about the Gothic in books and movies, followed by a memoir about high school, and scattered in between essays about everything else I'd ever been interested in including playing pickup basketball. How could I draw any kind of pattern with those particular dots? At best, I looked like an amateur, a well-heeled dilettante. But pattern? Map to a life— and mine was well more than half done I suppose—that was hard to find. It was as though a child had tossed a handful (a rather large handful, for I was nothing if not productive) of those stick-on stars, gold and red and blue and (I'm afraid at times) black, onto his playroom floor, let them fall where they might. "You're all over the place." Was that really me?

My friend was anything but all over the place. One of his books grew out of the next in a progression both logical and illuminating. He had started with one poet—a great one. And what he had learned meditating on that giant, he took into the field of poetry in general. Now this was someone who knew how to conduct a career—and maybe even a life. For the process of growth that is the unfolding of literary talents and interest is a perfectly fine model for the expansion of a life, and my friend's life had expanded most successfully.

And I? I was all over the place, wasn't I? It seemed I had nothing like Pollan's dialectic of culture and nature to work through in its many forms. And, a professor myself, I possessed nothing like my professor friend's trajectory of intellectual growth. Or so it then seemed to me.

Was there anything that held my work together—or was it just a repeated rattling and tossing of the dice? Did my writing (did I?) have an overall point?

Sometimes the best answers are the most obvious—and also, as in this case, the strangest. I hated school for a long time. Middle school, high school: about seven years of it were for me stretches of desert alternating with pits of muck. I hated it. I hated the teachers and the books they gave us and the way the books talked to us and the way the teachers talked about them. School was prison. I sensed that and when I heard it confirmed one day by the writer Ken Kesey, a real writer, I felt completely justified in my view. School was prison and I had been a seven-year convict.

But later when I looked across the terrain of my writing, one fact came clear. I was always writing, in one way or another, about education. I was writing mostly about individual education. I was interested in, and often moved by, the way an individual takes herself or himself in hand and goes about making changes. We're all given a life by nature; and we're all subjected to the influence of culture. But for some of us—for many I'd guess—the culture we're given by our parents and by our churches and by our towns and by our schools (by our schools, in particular!) isn't good enough. That kind of education doesn't put us in a satisfying relation to life and to others. So we've got to strike out for ourselves.

It's not that we don't have teachers; everyone needs teachers. But ours aren't the usual pedagogues, the ones who stand at the front of the class and bore us into semicomas. Our teachers are the ones we seek out. Sometimes they're attached to institutions, sure; but very often they're not. Our teachers can surprise us. Plato was a teacher for me, and Shakespeare too (though it took years to figure out what I'd learned from them). The game of football was a teacher of mine (and I've written about how) back when I was in my teens. Now the game of basketball, pickup basketball (one of the most democratic and elevating pursuits you can find in America now I think) is a teacher of mine, too. It's very good for someone who stands at the front of a class and can readily be mistaken for an unflappable authority to spend time doing something he loves but is at best so-so at.

I educated myself in my own fashion, freestyle, as Augie March says. But the process of education didn't only involve reading such and such a book or playing a sport or having two children (and so going back to school two more times than I might have liked). It also meant writing about those experiences. Because I don't think education is complete, truly complete, until you have turned your significant experiences into words and seen what the words might reveal to you. And since experience continues, there is always the possibility for further education, as you turn what's happened to you (and what you've made happen) into more sentences.

I wanted to do this for myself—educate myself through and in the medium of words. And I wanted—I'm still answering my friend here, though I'm answering myself, too—to offer the chance to others. A tenet of mine is that if you only take the paths that are unrolled before you, by the authorities, you may well be righteously screwed. There is a yellow brick road for you, I think, but you have to get to work and find it yourself. Most of the public signposts are lies; most of the guides are deceivers. Thoreau is right when he tells us there's not much to learn from most of the old: they've messed up their lives to unendurable degrees and are now seeking the appearance of redemption by posing as guides to others.

Don't I risk posing as that sort of guide? (Horrors compounded.) I risk it I suppose, but really I want to say one thing: Here's what worked, or half worked for me. What's going to do it for you? Something will. Something has to make the lives of usually quiet and occasionally noisy desperation most of us lead a little better than they are. By reading, by traveling, by playing sports, by talking to people, and by listening, you can gather the resources to make a life of your own. (That, in condensed terms, is the answer to the question: Why read?) By taking your experience and making it into words you solidify and define what you've acquired and make it the basis for further growth. And maybe you inspire a few others along the way to do the same for themselves. (That, in condensed terms, is the answer to the question: Why write?) And when you see that life isn't only about the individual (you) but about the group and community and you decide you want to live in a country and world where people aren't being produced like machines in a factory, then you do what you can do to spread the word about the marvelous chances there are to stop listening to the nonsense that's in the papers and on TV and burbling on the Internet and get in contact with the best that's known and thought (and played and sung), then you can contemplate being a teacher, one who teaches by example (flawed and funny, I hope) and not by edict. You think you'd like to stop trying to blow solos and want to be part of a jazz band where everyone can play something fresh and people like playing backup almost as much as they like standing out front and blasting away. (That, in compressed terms, is the answer to the question: Why teach?)

So you write books about education rather than about nature and culture or about the development of poetry. And (look!) your work isn't all over the place. And even if the constellation that the books and essays make doesn't glow with diamond brightness in the writers' night sky, there it is—and maybe it's still waiting to be completed. Maybe it lacks a star or two or three, sharper than the rest, more interesting to contemplate, and for others a modest but sure guide through the territory of their lives.

TO HAVE THE LAST WORD

L ET'S SAY, SHIFTING the metaphor away from constellations
and to something more duly modest, that the writer's career
looks something like a sentence. Every significant work is for
him, for her, a word, or a set of words. All good things must
come to an end and even the best of sentences must find a
period. (Though there are times when reading Proust, say, one
might doubt that this is so.) In this case, what is the period but
the writer's last word?

To be sure, anyone can write—or speak—his own epitaph.
But a writer is likely someone who will ponder those last words.
He wants to mold them, shape them, get them just right. He
wants a final perfection. I cannot imagine that Goethe's final
cry was entirely unconceived until the moment of articulation:
More light! And I would be very surprised to find that the
words on Yeats's tombstone or Keats's grave were but a moment's
thought. "Cast a cold eye on life, on death," it says on Yeats's
stone. Then the final leap: "Horseman, pass by." You could
spend a profitable enough week pondering that inscription in
the light of Yeats's life and work. Keats's will break your heart if

you have a heart to break (and know something about his life and early death). "Here lies one whose name was writ in water." Not true, though: ultimately not true, which I suspect is precisely what Keats hoped when he wrote it. He did confess in a letter that he believed he would be "among the English poets." "He is," Matthew Arnold said of him, hyperbolically but generously, "He is with Shakespeare."

Famous last words! Are there any that are better than Oscar Wilde's? He is in disgrace, having served time for (what comes down to) being homosexual. He has lost his money, his reputation, and his position. His name is a synonym for depravity all through England. He's exiled in Paris and he is sick, badly sick. Looking around his shabby chamber he focuses on the cracked and broken crockery on the shelf, always the aesthete, always the connoisseur par excellence, utters the immortal words: "This wallpaper and I are fighting a duel to the death. Either it goes or I do."

Thoreau departs with the words: Moose. Indian. Or perhaps it was: Indian. Moose. Emerson in his grand but equivocal eulogy for Thoreau says that Thoreau loved an encounter with a "good Indian." That is, one who could swap lore with him about where trout could be caught in August and how to set a trap for beaver and where the best huckleberries might be found. Thoreau was a learner all of his life, much like Emerson. But Thoreau came to the end of it having put forward a lean but complete vision of his philosophy in *Walden*—assuming that by philosophy you mean how to live, and live wisely. A moose sighted at the pond would have been a major event to HDT, one to brood on and take pleasure from for many days to come. Moose. Indian. Thoreau was maybe the first real American, and maybe the only one. White as he was, he kept the legacy of nature (moose) and the natives who got here first (Indians) and then extended them to himself and his kind. In *Walden*, maybe the best American book (*Leaves of Grass* is not a book but a vision quest; *Moby-Dick* is a prophetic rapture), Thoreau says he aspires to fuse within himself the hardihood and resourcefulness of the savage with the refinement of the civilized man. It's surprising how much, for instance, Thoreau admired the railroad.

James Joyce ended by asking those he was leaving on earth and maybe too those celestial spirits he would meet in heaven a direct question: Does nobody understand? Surely he was thinking of *Finnegans Wake* and of *Ulysses* and maybe of his own strange nature, simultaneously so earthy and refined. Tolstoy left the world talking about his love for all things living and prophesying the fulfillment of the vision of Jesus. Not long before, he had repudiated almost all of his great works because they traduced the message of the Gospels.

The list of writers' last words goes on and will until it touches infinity and then rolls past it. But the question remains: Why are writers given to final pronouncements? Why do they seem to study and craft and refine their last words? What's the attraction to putting their own period at the end of the sentence that has been their lives and works?

One thinks of a grand pronouncement by Oscar Wilde—my candidate for the most sublime of last wordsmiths. Wilde's line about how either the wallpaper goes or he does is perfect. It condenses his aestheticism, his desperation, his claims to courage, and his capacity to exalt himself by diminishing himself.

Wilde said many other memorable things of course. A favorite of mine is very simple: "Most people," Wilde said, "are other people." Now what exactly does that mean? One can only speculate. But—one might say that most people make themselves over in the image of the crowd. They don't want to be noticed, don't want to be heard. (Unless it is anonymously, online: then look out.) They want to conform. Most people share their values and their virtues and their vices, too, with other people. They are copies of replicas of facsimiles. They pick up their senses of self from school and church and home and the neighborhood and the movies and the Internet and then have done with it. They are echoes of echoes, shadows of shadows. Writers may be these things too in the end, but they do not wish to be. If there's a flaw in the die that stamps them, they will struggle to make a virtue of it. They do not want their identities conferred by others; they will not be beholden to newspapers for who they are. They will write their story lines, and in the end they will write their obituaries, too. The genre of the self-elegy in modern poetry is anything but a depleted one.

Most people are other people. But some refuse the offer to be anything other than they are or aspire to be. They want to appropriate the discourse, as they say in lit theory 101. It matters to them that they make their own record even up to the last possible moment and maybe even beyond. The poet Mark Strand had what he thought a splendid moneymaking idea— but maybe it was more than that. It was an innovation in grave-yard design. Headstones would be equipped with what amounted to an archive. And when you put a few dollars into the appropriate slot, or swiped your credit card, or (down the line) let the stone's apparatus read the bar code tattooed on your wrist at birth, you could get an encounter with the deceased. Here comes his favorite song right at you, then a passage from the book he loved best, a dozen or so of the jokes he laughed loudest at, then maybe his own last words, all recorded and sent your way. Maybe in time you could access videos. So much better than cold stone: the deceased could be there at your fingertips, or at the edge of your credit card. The proceeds? Those would go to the family in addition to (or in lieu of) any material legacy available at moment of departure. What is to be said about this idea? Much. But I'll simply observe that only a writer could have had it. If Mark Strand created such a final installation, I'd be there to take it in, credit card in hand.

Change the trope a bit. What is a book but a record of the spirit over a period of time in the writer's life? (What is a good book I mean.) So if you've created a span of books, you've created a span of memorials—call them grave markers if you like—and you can look back over them as the days wind down. But inside each one is not death but life, or all the life you might have been able to muster at the time. That life becomes manifest when the book is opened by someone else down the line. And that life is augmented when your book becomes an inspiration or a goad to another writer—or someone who wishes to be one. Writers can be competitive as Formula One drivers, sure, but beneath that there's a sense of unanimity or hopefulness that flows from one to the other, as through members of a team.

In a sense, Mark Strand's crazy dream is already alive—in that every book that's any good is likely to be full of the writer's best wisdom and even his favorite jokes and the scraps of a song or two. Open one and see. And if the book stays quiet for long years and no one taps on its door, still there is hope. The spirit is open-eyed in there (if the book is a good one) ready to jump out and perform its white magic in the world. Who cannot date a new epoch in his life to the reading of a book? The life that is enshrined in a good book waits there patiently for the right reader or readers to come along and be lifted out of the doldrums and take sail with a fresh wind. The old writer is reborn in the spirit of the new. And that is reincarnation— and immortality on the small scale, or at least as close as most any of us is likely to come.

A NOTE ON THE AUTHOR

Mark Edmundson teaches at the University of Virginia, where he is a University Professor. A prizewinning scholar, he is also the author of *Why Teach?*, *Why Read?*, *Teacher*, *The Death of Sigmund Freud*, *The Fine Wisdom and Perfect Teachings of the Kings of Rock and Roll* and *Literature Against Philosophy: Plato to Derrida*, among other books. His writing has appeared in such publications as the *Los Angeles Review of Books,* the *New York Times Magazine*, the *Chronicle of Higher Education*, the *Nation*, the *American Scholar, London Review of Books, Raritan*, and *Harper's Magazine*. He lives in Batesville, Virginia.